ONCE UPON A TIME, BITCHES

Design Your Fairytale Life, Control Your Destiny, and Become the Hero in Your Story

BRANDEN LANETTE

Published by

SHORT BOOKS. BIG IDEAS.

www.SuccessIn100Pages.com

ISBN 978-1-947814-86-8

LEGAL DISCLAIMER:

DEDICATION:

This book is dedicated to my Prince Charming (Benjamin), my kids (Shaylynn, Jezra, Malachi, Isaiah, Zaden and Alexandria), and to *The Whisper* that kept telling me there was more.

WARNING:

This book contains a fair amount of what some people consider to be foul language (you know, like the occasional *fuck-this* and *you've-got-to-be-shitting-me that*) plus an enormous amount of explicit honesty (which can be more difficult for some people to tolerate than a few curse words).

But my publisher wants you to know that, at no time, is anyone promoting the irresponsible use of swear words. As such, every shit, fuck, bitch and bastard in this book has been used intentionally, appropriately and with the utmost care.

-Branden LaNette

(while flossing my teeth and searching for a fresh roll of toilet paper)

ANOTHER WARNING:

I probably need to address the use of the word *"bitch"* in the title and at various times throughout the book.

The *Urban Dictionary* considers the word bitch to be one of the most versatile words in the English language, used to express a multitude of emotions:

Anger *("Bitch makes me so damn mad")*...

Envy *("That bitch has a Birkin bag?")*...

Horror *("You scared the living hell out of me, bitch")*...

Warning *("Don't test me, bitch")*...

Awesomeness *("That party was bitchin'")*...

Difficulty *("Life's a bitch")*...

And an endless list of other uses.

But *"bitch"* can also be used to suggest an empowered, assertive woman.

That is the way it is intended here.

(BTW: Do you know who invented the word bitch? Shakespeare! I shit you not.)

OH, SHIT, ONE LAST WARNING:

Unless you checked this book out at the library or it was "gifted" to you, you laid out hard-earned cash to read what I have to say. So, thanks.

But what I really need from you is something more valuable than money—*I need you to trust me.* And to have faith that nothing I'll be sharing is designed to hurt you. It is designed to create emotional and financial freedom and save your damn life—maybe even to save you from yourself, like I have finally done.

You may not agree with everything I have to say, but the most important takeaway is that YOU have to be your own fucking hero. No more damsel-locked-in-a-tower waiting for some guy to climb your Rapunzel-length-hair bullshit. If the words *please save me* are currently in your vocabulary, get them the fuck out of there right now.

I am going to make you uncomfortable.

Back out now if you aren't ready.

Shit is about to get real, bitches...

INTRODUCTION

A Wee Bit of Intro Before We Head Into the Forest

T hey say the professional way to start any book is with an introduction. So, okay, let me introduce myself:

I am Branden.

I know, the name doesn't exactly fit with the gorgeous face planted on the cover of this book, but I got over it. So will you.

I am a superhero queen. No cape, no crown, just a stunning "mom bod" with droopy boobs and stretch marks like most of my fellow *hero queens* out there.

Don't get me wrong, dads can be heroes, too. I am married to my prince charming: my second husband, but my first love. More on that later. And, just so we're clear (before I dish out all the juicy details), he is off the market. He is mine, mine, mine, all mine.

We have a fairytale life, prince charming and me. We never fight. Our lives are perfect.

We have six children (wait, let me count again: *one, two, three...* yep, six) each of them flawless and perfectly behaved. Even better, we were born into some serious cash and have never struggled financially. Birds sing a chorus, and animals gather when we walk outside.

(Insert eye-roll emoji here)...

Because if you believe that shit is true for *anyone*, then you're living on a different planet.

I'm Nothing Special...

In many ways, I'm nothing special, pretty much like most everyone. Then again, after years of soul-searching and intense personal development, I know I'm totally special and wildly awesome.

Sometimes witty, full of sarcasm. Loud, bratty, and I love attention. Obviously. But there are still periods where I struggle, just trying to fucking survive. Or stay on task. Make no mistake, I'm writing this book to help you, but it's pretty therapeutic for me, too.

I've made tons of mistakes and taken the wrong turn multiple times in my life, yet—while I wasn't born with magical powers or superhuman intelligence—I am smart as fuck. I've accepted that about myself now, even though I didn't used to.

The world I used to live in was one in which everything and everybody were trying to hold me down (at least that's what I thought). Today, things are different.

I have found my passion and am finally living an incredible life—glamorous and sexy. If screaming kids and puppy poop is sexy to you, then you can probably relate.

...Yet I'm Extraordinary, Too

 s I just explained, I am—in the grand scheme of things—nothing special. Yet, at the same time, I've accepted that I am pretty damn extraordinary. No different than you, right? *Right?*

You are extraordinary, too. You know that, don't you? If not, I'm going to do everything within my power to make sure that—by the end of this book—you understand just how special and extraordinary and powerful you really are.

Every Princess Has an Origin Story.
This Is Mine.

L et me say that I'd rather *not* tell you my story. Not here, especially in print for all the world to see. Hell, I'd rather not tell it anywhere!

Besides, this book isn't really about me.

It's about you.

But I know that if I'm unwilling to open up and share my story with you, then where's the trust? So I've decided to trust you, even though we've never met, and tell you my story: all of it, no holds barred. And who knows, maybe someday we'll meet and you can tell me yours.

Now, don't worry, I have no intention of writing my full autobiography here, and trust me when I tell you that I'm skipping over tons of juicy shit that would literally curl your hair (yes, there too).

Simply put, my childhood wasn't good. I didn't have it easy. Now, this is where you roll your eyes and say, *"Who does, Branden?"* And you'd be right, because it's true. No one goes through childhood without enduring some kind of trauma. Even trust-fund babies experience pain, I imagine (a form of struggle I admittedly have no experience with but I'm sure they struggle, nonetheless).

At the core of *my* struggle was the fact that I was rejected by my mother. Notice I didn't say I *felt* rejected by my mother, which would mean I *interpreted* it that way. The rejection I experienced isn't some childhood interpretation of events. I *was* rejected by her.

The rejection was *real.*

And it hurt.

Looking back now, trying to make sense of how she could be so cruel, so unloving and so distant, I've come to understand that I was simply too much for her to handle. To be clear, I'm not saying it was my fault. Nor am I saying it was hers.

It was what it was.

I did not live with my mom after the age of 12. I basically couch-surfed between 12 and 15, and I worked my ass off to ensure I always had a place to live, usually being supported by my friends' parents. I'm not proud.

And then I got in with the wrong crowd.

I was the wrong crowd.

I got involved with drugs. No excuse. But it dulled the pain.

My mom surrendered me to the court system at the age of 14. I was serving a two-year juvenile commitment sentence. What does that mean exactly? Well, more stuff I'm not proud of. I was on probation for keying a car and a drug overdose violated it.

I was constantly on the run. Running from what? Everything. Running to where? Anywhere. At a court hearing, my mom stood up and gave up her rights. She gave up her rights to me, and I became a ward of the state.

Finally, at 15, still in a horrible relationship with my mom (her wanting nothing to do with me), I surrendered any hope she'd become the mom I dreamed of having. I also made the decision to become legally emancipated.

Out There, On My Own

Here I was, out on my own—emancipated, in an apartment at the age of 16—with no examples of unconditional love or life lessons, no money management, no direction and working full time to support myself.

One of the requirements for emancipation was to get my GED, so I went in and took the test.

For those of you who have no idea what a GED is, it's an equivalency certificate that you get by taking a test, the purpose of which is to serve as a substitute for a high school diploma. That's correct, I didn't finish school. I think it's fair to say most of you reading this already have one up on me.

I was winging it.

And boy did I fuck things up, over and over again. I made horrible relationship choices (more on that later), had no friends, and in the rare situation where I *did* make a friend, I never kept them for long. I was a lone wolf who never fit in, with little prospects for a decent future.

But I Had a Plan...

As truly fucked up as I was, I still had hope. Actually, I had something better than hope. I had a plan.

With my GED, I was able to enroll in college and pursue a degree in criminal justice, which seemed appropriate considering I'd spent a lot of time in detention centers as a kid. To this day, I'm not entirely sure how I pulled this off.

Then I got arrested. At 16, I was arrested as an adult because I was on "adult parole" since I emancipated early, after being committed to the juvenile justice system.

(I know I can barely keep it straight either.)

Anyway, this arrest resulted in a humiliating *strip search* which was conducted, ironically, by a college classmate I sat next to every day in school.

It was a case of being in the wrong place at the wrong time, but I was innocent and never charged.

Still, going back to class and facing the humiliation of sitting side by side with my law-abiding classmates was out of the question. I simply couldn't face it. And getting accepted to another college seemed unlikely. So I did the only thing I could think to do—I changed my major—and decided to become a psychologist.

Yes, a psychologist.

Which was totally insane, of course, considering how fucked up I was. But, at that time, it somehow made sense. It didn't just make sense, it was brilliant.

As a psychologist, I could sit behind a big oak desk, using it as a shield to hide to my shame and embarrassment, holding a pen in my hand like a sword, and making my living listening to unhappy rich people complain about the life I'd always dreamed of for myself. Like I said, it was a brilliant idea!

So I continued in and out of college classes, thinking this in and of itself was success, or at least good enough. But I never really committed with my heart. I had no direction.

At least I was an amazing employee. Which was good since I was working three jobs (and taking drugs to stay awake since I worked pretty much all the time). I also think that was part of the reason I always stayed stuck, I was comfortable and so valued at these places, I never trusted myself to dream big.

Fast forward to my next smart move.

Is This Prince Charming? Can I See an ID?

I met my first husband when I was 18 and by the time I was 19, were living together as common-law husband and wife. I finally had a partner but for some reason, I still felt empty. Was this my prince charming?

I didn't know. Clearly, I was still screwed up. I needed a purpose.

And then it hit me: There had to be someone out there who was even more fucked up than I was—some other lost kid who just needed a fucking chance.

So, I did what any totally fucked up young woman with no workable vision or plans for a future would do—I decided to become a foster parent to kids with bad attitudes who were struggling like I was. And that's what I did.

At the tender age of 21, still a child in so many ways myself, I became a foster parent to two young, troubled boys. Right around this time, I got pregnant and my supposed prince charming and I split and got a divorce—right before I had my first daughter.

But I discovered something: Helping those kids, providing them with a home and giving an unconditional fuck about them, gave me purpose and set my heart on fire. I finally had a clear mission, which was to be the mother I'd never had. And that's what I did.

We all have a gift, and being a mom is mine. I give my all. Finding my joy in the life of a mommy is my jam above all else. And with that said, a year later, another gift arrived in the form of a second daughter.

So there I was, stubbornly and independently living by myself as a foster parent and the bio mom to two young girls. My ex and I were off and on during this whole time. You know: one of those fucked up, destructive, rollercoaster relationships that you know in your heart you should not be in? That was it.

So, what do you think I did?

Kissing the Same Frog Twice

I remarried him.

I shit you not.

Less than three years after the divorce was final, I remarried my ex. Yes, I kissed the same fucking frog twice! Can you fucking believe it? You'd think after I kissed that frog the first time, and he turned out to be a toad rather than a prince, I'd have learned my lesson. Nope. (Remember, this is the old Branden we're talking about. I was a real slow learner).

Now, I want to make sure you've got the picture. Here I was:

- *A foster mom to two kids...*
- *With a baby and a toddler of my own...*
- *Still taking classes I didn't care about...*
- *With no prospects for a promising future...*
- *Dreaming of being a published author...*
- *Remarried to the guy I'd divorced once before...*
- *And with another baby on the way (number three!)*

Something had to give.

And it did.

After several years as a foster parent the situation changed. Besides the normal stresses of school, marriage and being a parent to my own kids, issues arose with my role as foster parent.

For one thing, I became weary with the foster care system—a system that was very difficult to navigate and deal with. Spending years fighting with caseworkers who shrugged and said their *hands were tied,* and with constant battles with judges, made me want to pull my hair out. I couldn't believe how screwed up the system was.

Admittedly, my poor taste in husbands didn't help, especially when he had to cop a plea to a felony theft charge, which looked terrible on paperwork with my foster parent agency. How could it not?

In any case, it all turned out to be more than I could handle. (Duh.) I needed to make a choice. A painful one. So after seven years, my role as a foster parent came to a heartbreaking end.

My job now became being the best fucking mom I could for *my* babies. It was all I had control over. It was the hardest thing I've ever done, but I had to set two foster kids free, kids I thought would be with me forever.

I took it hard and blamed myself for the failure.

Over the years, I've had people tell me what a saint I was for taking on the role of foster parent to those kids in the first place. And to the degree that a couple kids were given hope for a least a little while (and with any luck think of me with a degree of gratitude), I feel blessed.

The Next Chapter, No Fairytale

fter my husband got fired from his job (you won't fucking believe why: He Googled where the president lived from his office at work, and they fired him), we moved into my dad's house, and I had my first son.

Six months later, we threw a dart in the map and joked about moving to Michigan. So, we loaded the U-Haul and three kids and drove from Colorado to a place we'd never been, with no jobs, no place to live, and not another human being that we knew.

We were trying to get rid of family drama. As a teen who spent her life running, why wouldn't I do that as an adult?

At this point in the story, my little girls were 7 and 8, and my baby boys were 3 and 1 (that's four kids now, in case you're counting). And to fill in my "spare" time, I was trying to write my book.

I spent hours every day, pounding the keyboard and querying agents, while homeschooling our kids. And, because we were short on cash, I was also moonlighting as a bartender to help pay the bills.

Now, as it turned out, bartending is a natural gift of mine. And though I was just short of a bachelor's degree, I was able to use my almost-psychology-degree, combined with my awesome wit and charm behind that bar.

(Dear God, the stories I could tell you about from the things I saw from behind that bar—another book for another time, perhaps. And if you are interested, I have an awesome recipe for a drink I call the Plan B. If you're a cool cat, hit me up someday and I'll tell you how it's made. Yes, I know my alcohol!)

It was while bartending that I got to watch thousands of people from all walks of life. I watched the successful people, the ones I thought I wanted to be, fight the same demons I was struggling with.

I watched unsuccessful people remain oblivious to the power they had to break the cycle of their self-destructive traps. And then there was me, pouring drinks and doing my best Billy Joel, wondering, *"Fuck, what in the hell are you doing here?"*

I watched people having good and bad days, like we all do. Which is when I realized: *We are all the same.* We are *all* just trying to make it through life the best way we know how.

Wishing for Things to Change

Before I make it sound like everyone on the other side of the bar was fucked up and I wasn't, let me set the record straight: I was still just *wishing* for shit to happen...

- *Wishing I had more money...*

- *Wishing I could stop hearing "no" from agents and publishers and I could make a million dollars overnight as a best-selling author...*

- *Wishing my marriage wasn't shit...*

- *Wishing I could just be home with my kids 24/7...*

- *Wishing I wasn't working in a smelly bar, getting my ass pinched (or worse) by poor-tipping jerkoffs...*

- *Wishing someone would ride in on a white horse and take a fucking chance on a nobody and make my dreams come true.*

Yes, I spent a lot of time wishing for things to happen. But the truth was, I wasn't doing anything to *make* them happen. I'd spent years doing my best to cope, fighting with my ex-husband every minute of every damn day while juggling all the other areas of my life, work and school and also struggling to be a good mother to my kids and provide them a loving home—all of it wearing me to exhaustion and near insanity.

"There Is More"

As crazy and out of control I had let my life become, I kept hearing a voice in the back of my mind—not a voice actually, but more of a whisper.

And the voice said:

"There is more."

At first, I ignored it. I'd been through a lot already: Life had thrown me a lot of curve balls. But the voice kept whispering...

"There is more."

I felt like Kevin Costner (but with boobs), standing in a corn field in Iowa.

More?

Fuck you, voice—I *can't* do more.

This was back when I was giving my baby girls everything I had—*how could there be more?*

But the voice kept at it with its annoying constant whisper.

"There is more."

Damn it, voice. Knock it off, huh?

"There is more."

Finally I threw up my hands and decided to play along. *"Okay, voice, more what?"* Was there more I was supposed to *give?* I wasn't capable of doing more (at least I didn't think I could, not at that time in my life). Maybe there was more I was supposed to *get.* Getting more sounded really good.

The Voice Wouldn't Go Away

There would be periods of time when the voice would go away, and, suddenly...

"There is more."

"Okay, whisper, now you're starting to piss me off," I raged. No matter how much vodka I drowned myself in, the damn voice inside my head would not shut up. Finally, I couldn't take it anymore.

One night, I literally lost it. Standing naked and alone in my bathroom, with tears streaming down my face looking at myself in the mirror, I released a primal scream and shouted, *"Okay, I'm ready! Do you hear me? I'm ready! Just tell me what you fucking want from me!"*

Eventually, I realized the same thing Kevin Costner discovered in "Field of Dreams": *the voice was mine all along.*

And what did it want from me? More accurately, what did *I* want from myself?

There was only *one* answer. One *word* that was the answer to everything. One *thing* that described not only what I wanted more of, but what everybody wants more of.

And that thing was...

Not just happiness. *I wanted to experience joy* (yes, there is a difference). And from that low place, I discovered how to turn hardship into happiness and pain into fuel for achievement.

And let me tell you—if a fucked up, heavily inked bitch with a boy's name like me can find more joy in her life, then so can you.

Joy vs. Happiness

What's the difference between joy and happiness? Aren't they the same thing? No, they are not.

Most people spend their lives searching for ways to make themselves happy. Which is fine, I guess. Kind of. The problem is that happiness is temporary and fleeting. And it requires external stuff, things from outside us, and the quest for more stuff is killing us.

Enough with "stuff" already.

The reality, when I think about it, is that stuff has never made me truly happy. And when it *did* make me happy, it only made me happy for a moment or two. A couple days, tops. Sound familiar?

Buying a new car makes just about anyone happy. But a month later? You barely even notice. Same thing goes for clothes, jewelry, and shoes. Don't get me wrong: I dig buying a cool pair of shoes just as much as the next girl, but did any pair of Jimmy Choo's ever bring me a sense of eternal, lasting joy?

Fuck, no.

I demand joy from everything I do and every dollar I spend. And I'm willing to work for it. Think of it as a continuum, like this:

Miserable <<< Unhappy <<< □ >>> Happy >>> Joyful

No one wants to be miserable, and they'll jump through just about any hoop to move to the right. The problem, for most people, is they get stuck in a state of unhappiness.

They never get to the other side of the equation.

And if they do, they stop at happy.

A Quest for Joy

I've stopped trying to find happiness. Instead, I'm on a constant quest for things that bring me joy.

To fully understand what I'm trying to say, here are some examples I've written for myself:

- Happiness is a job that pays the bills. *Joy is having a career you love.*

- Happiness is being liked by strangers. *Joy is liking yourself.*

- Happiness is collecting a houseful of dumbass dogs because it seemed like a good idea at the time. *Joy is finding a way to ditch the entire pack without breaking my kid's hearts.*

- Happiness is having enough money to go on vacation. *Joy is freedom.*

- Happiness is going on social media and seeing several nice comments and that no one is trolling you. *Joy is not checking social media because you simply don't give fuck what anyone thinks, good or bad.*

- Happiness is having someone take care of you. *Joy is knowing that you are in control of your destiny and able to take care of yourself.*

Not someone else. *You.*

Admittedly, it can be difficult to shift from seeking our next happiness-hit to a quest for things with deeper meaning.

And while meditation is great for creating inner peace and quieting the constant chatter in your head, I've found there are a number of other things that must be done to reach the joy-filled place we all want to arrive at eventually.

Seven things, to be precise. I call them my *Seven Maxims.*

The Seven Maxims

The use of the word *maxim* is not a reference to the men's magazine. It's a term that comes from medieval Latin, referring to *pithy yet important rules or truths*. Think of me as a tattooed Snow White with Seven Maxims rather than dwarfs.

The balance of this book is dedicated to the seven maxims I have discovered and developed during my quest for a joyful fairytale life—a journey I am still on to this day.

I promise that if you apply these timeless truths, they will bring you that rarest of things...

I'm talking joy, bitches...

Motherfucking Joy.

(cue the cheesy sappy music and birds chirping)

Now, would someone please tell those fucking birds to shut the hell up because we've got work to do.

Branden's Magical Maxim #1
for Manifesting a Fairytale Life:

Realize that no one is coming to save you. You have to save yourself.

#OUATB

Ever since I was 8 years old, I dreamed of an easy life. The problem with my dream? I expected that fairytale life to be handed to me. And when it wasn't, I decided that fairytales were bullshit. Not that you can't have a fairytale life—you can. What I understand now, however, is that to get a fairytale life, you'd better be willing to work your Cinderella-ass off for it.

Still, I held on to the fantasy of having an easy life handed to me. I wanted to be *saved*. To be specific, I thought I needed a *guy* to be my hero. So I went about trying to find one.

I dated a lot of guys.

Lots of guys.

But as they came and went, I always ended up disappointed. Not a single one of them ever made my life easier. Things weren't going the way I'd planned. WTF? Hadn't anyone read the fucking script? It was right there on page 43:

> *"Tall handsome guy with tight ass, great pecs*
> *and a 124-foot yacht named "Shitload of Cash"*
> *enters stage-left and sweeps Branden off her feet,*
> *and they sail off to Barbados."*

Even in my adult years, I would find myself just wishing—not just for prince charming to appear (which he eventually did in the form of my husband, minus the yacht and gobs of cash) but wishing for things in every area of my life. Even today, in my writing/coaching career, I find myself drifting into wish-mode: *Why isn't this easier? Why can't things just take off and grow overnight? Is it always going to be this hard?*

And when it comes to parenting, it's the same thing. *Why can't parenting just be easy?* And in my marriage, too: *Why do I have to keep asking for things?* Can't my husband just read my fucking mind?

The Moment of Realization

ne day I—still 8 years old—had the most terror-filled realization in a simple yet profound truth:

No one is coming to save you.

Fuck.

No one is coming to rescue me.

Ever?

My heart broke. More like shattered. Yet, after taking some time to mentally digest this fact, I found this realization liberating somehow. Why was this liberating? Because it meant I could stop waiting for something outside myself for my salvation.

It put *me* in control.

Newsflash, bitches: *No one is coming to save you, either.* Get it? *No. One. Is. Coming.* You're going to have to save yourself.

Part of me feels like I should apologize for slapping you across the face so early with this crushing yet obvious truth. After all, you may not need slapping in this area. Then again, you might.

Fair warning, there's a lot more bitch-slapping in the pages to come. And to be completely honest, the *first* bitch I slapped was myself. (To be clear, you may not need slapping in this area. Then again, you might. Hey, if the glass slipper fits...)

Victim, Villain, Hero

Think about this: Every story you've ever been told, be it movie, musical, novel, fairytale, whatever—revolves around one critical element and three major characters.

The critical element every story has is:

Conflict.

It's the first thing every creative writing teacher tells their students they need to include to create a compelling tale, right? *No conflict, no story.*

Airplane takes off, flies to its destination, and lands safely does not make for an entertaining story. There's no conflict. Now, insert bomb (or empty alcohol cart), and you've got a story. In my case, I had conflict coming out of my ass.

Next, the story requires three major characters:

1. **Victim** (the person who has been wronged, damaged and/or is in danger)

2. **Villain** (the person or entity who has done or is about to do the dastardly deed), and the...

3. **Hero** (the person who is going to come to the victim's rescue).

Every story has conflict and all three characters. For example, let's look at one of the most well-known fairytales of all time: "Cinderella."

The three major roles needed for any great story are all present in the "Cinderella" tale. They are:

1. Victim: *(Cinderella)*

2. Villain/Villains: *(the evil stepmother and horribly abusive stepsisters)*

3. And the Hero?

It's a great question. Who *is* the hero of the "Cinderella" tale? Now, before you're tempted to quickly throw out an answer, let's do a quick refresher of the original, old-school (non-Disney) version:

Act One:

Our victim, Cinderella, lives with her horribly cruel and abusive stepsisters, Clorinda and Tisbe, who dump on her day and night by making her cook and clean, then reward her by making her sleep in the cinders by the fireplace (hence the name *Cinder*-ella). One day, a beggar arrives at the cottage, begging for food. The stepsisters run away, repulsed by the lowly creature. But Cinderella? She sees him as a human, like her, so she offers him something to eat and drink. This is where the wheels of *karma* start turning and the beggar pledges to return the kind deed in the future.

Soon thereafter, an invitation to a ball at the castle arrives. Turns out, the prince is looking to find a wife (which would make just about anyone ask, *"What-in-the-fuck-are-the-chances-of-that?"*). Anyway, as you might suspect, the stepsisters are all over this shit and start getting ready for the big shindig. When Cinderella asks if she can go, everybody has a good laugh. *"You? At the ball? Get real, girl!"* they scoff.

Cinderella takes the *dis* in stride since her entire life has been nothing but *dis*appointment. She's sad, but she's helpless to do anything about it and soon falls asleep by the fire.

Act Two:

Cinderella's fairy godmother makes her entrance and a few *bibbidi-bobbidi-boos* later, she's transformed into a beautiful princess. Cinderella digs the free makeover but isn't sure going to the ball is a good idea. What if her stepsisters recognize her? No problem! Turns out the fairy godmother just happens to have a pair of magical glass slippers that will make Cinderella unrecognizable. But there's a catch!

The fairy godmother tells Cinderella she has to be home by midnight—if she's even a minute late, the spell will be broken.

Better take that shit seriously, bitch—rules are rules even in fairytales. So off she goes.

Meanwhile, at the castle, the prince gets his panties in wad, worried that the women who come to the ball might only be after his money *(ya think?)*. So, the prince and his page do a switcheroo and trade clothing. This way, any of the gold-digging bitches will think the prince is just a servant, and the servant is the prince, and tip their hand. It's brilliant!

Soon after their arrival, the stepsisters start fighting over the page (whom they believe to be the prince) and throw shade at the Prince (whom they assume to be a servant). Then Cinderella makes her entrance and, wouldn't ya' know it, the real prince falls head over heels for her. They dance, they flirt, and they sing (because singing is in every fairytale, at least after Hollywood gets a hold of it). Of course, Cinderella's having such a good time, she doesn't notice the minutes ticking away. Fuck! It's midnight!

Cinderella remembers the warning and bolts out of there, losing one of her slippers in the process. Fortunately, the prince retrieves it.

Act Three:

The prince sets off on a tour of the kingdom to find the owner of the shoe. But alas, it's too small for any of the women who try it on because, as you know, hot chicks all have small feet. When the prince finally arrives at the evil stepmother's house, the stepsisters each insist the slipper is theirs, but (of course) it doesn't fit. But it fits Cinderella perfectly! The prince promptly reveals his true identity, asks Cinderella to marry him, and they live (hold for it... hold for it...) happily ever after.

P.S. After all this, Cinderella forgives her sisters for being cruel bitches, just in case we didn't think she was perfect enough already. The End.

So, now that we've reviewed the story, I'll ask the question once again: *Who is the hero of the story?* Is it:

A. *The Prince*

B. *The Beggar*

C. *The Fairy Godmother*

Common sense says it's A. The Prince. After all, he's the one who saved her, right? But one could make the case it was B. the Beggar, since the beggar is the one who sent the invitation to the ball. Then again, maybe it's C. the Fairy Godmother. She's the one with the magic wand.

It's a trick question, because the real answer is D. None of the Above. Because the hero of the story is Cinderella.

Being the Hero

How is Cinderella the hero in "Cinderella"? First, the prince can't be the hero because he did nothing heroic. All the prince did was use his power to get the girl—what *he* wanted. He didn't set off on his quest to save Cinderella from her plight—*he did it for himself.* How does that make *him* the hero?

It doesn't.

And as far as the beggar and the fairy godmother go, neither of them saved Cinderella. Yes, you *could* make the case that they made it possible for Cinderella to *go* to the ball, but that's all they did—make it possible.

It was Cinderella herself who set the wheels in motion by treating the beggar with kindness, *and karma is a real thing, bitches.* You put enough good shit out there, some good shit is gonna come back around. Oh, and lest I forget to mention—Cinderella took a chance, got in the fucking carriage, and went to the damn dance. No way the prince meets Cinderella if she stays at home crying by the fireplace!

You want Prince Charming to find you? You want *anything* to go your way in life? You've got to do the three things Cinderella did:

1. *You've got to be kind (worthy of good karma)*

2. *You've got to be patient (remember, the universe works on its own schedule, not yours)*

And when opportunity finally *does* knock...

3. *You've got to open the door, accept the invitation, and show the fuck up!*

That's right, bitches. Show the fuck up.

Today's Princess Is Different

If you're paying attention, you can't help but notice the stereotypical adherence to gender roles. Princess is in danger. Prince saves her. Translation: *woman weak, man strong.* The end. But recently that has started to change. Thank God.

For example:

- There are two main characters in "Maleficent," Aurora and Maleficent, both of whom need help, and neither of which is saved by a prince.

- In "Tangled" (the modern update of the classic "Rapunzel"), Rapunzel doesn't need saving from the tower—in fact, she saves Finn not just once, but twice: first from a bar brawl, then later from drowning in a cave. In the end, we think Finn is dead, but she saves his life.

- In "Beauty and the Beast," Belle is released by the beast so she can go help her father but returns and saves the beast from the angry mob. In fact, the best scene of the movie is when the beast nearly dies (in her loving arms), and *her* love magically saves *him*. Belle doesn't need rescuing—Belle is the rescuer. Go Belle!

- In "Frozen," Anna not only isn't in love with a man, she uses her pure love to save her sister, Elsa.

- And what about "Mulan?" When Fa Mulan's father is injured, she dresses like a man and serves in the army in his place and becomes one of the best soldiers in the process! She saves tons of people from the Huns, including Li Shang, the captain, whom she's got the hots for. Fa is a female character with brains and brawn—who woulda thunk it?

- Finally, there's "Pocahontas," a free-spirited bitch if ever there was one. Does she need to be rescued by John Smith? Nope, *she* rescues *him*. And at the end of this movie, the princess and the prince (uh, captain) don't even end up together! Her family and friends were more important to her than he was.

Like Bob Dylan said, *the times they are a changin'.*

Deconstructing 'Pretty Woman'

Which brings us to "Pretty Woman," the 1990 hit movie starring Julia Roberts and Richard Gere. Remember how it ended?

If not, here's a quick refresher:

Interior—Vivian's Apartment—Day.

Vivian hears a car honking loudly outside. Music from the soprano solo from the opera, "La Traviata," begins to play, and Vivian walks to the window.

Vivian looks out and sees a limousine pulling up to the curb. She smiles when she sees it's Edward, flowers in hand. Vivian giggles, so happy that she's fighting back tears.

The perfect fucking ending. Roll credits? No, not yet.

There's a twist!

Edward sees that Vivian isn't coming down. Shit. He's going to have to climb the fire escape to the third floor and go get her—and (wouldn't you know) he's afraid of heights, cleverly established in Act I.

EDWARD

Had to be the top floor, right ?

VIVIAN

It's the best.

EDWARD

All right. I'm coming up.

Edward grabs the emergency ladder with the hook of his umbrella (always a nice touch if there's an umbrella around), pulls it down, and starts climbing, flowers clenched in his teeth. Up above, on the balcony, Vivian unties her hair, and it cascades down in slow motion as an off-screen fan blows (also a nice touch if you can pull it off).

Edward, though scared shitless, presses on (his back literally "against the wall") until he reaches the top. They move toward each other, their faces close now.

EDWARD:

So what happened after he climbed up the tower and rescued her?

(Wait for it... Wait for it...)

VIVIAN

She rescues him right back.

That's right—*she* rescues *him*. Edward is the one who needed rescuing all along. Edward is the victim. *Vivian is the hero!*

(They kiss passionately. Music from "La Traviata" fades. Cue the doves—no, wait, even better—cue a beach-dwelling Rastafarian.)

No More Waiting, Okay?

I'm not Freud and won't pretend to be (though I did study psychology for two years), so when I say this, it's mostly from the standpoint of awareness and common sense, but I believe we tend to sit back and wait for someone or something to save us as a matter of comfort. *We get comfortable with being the victim.* We get *comfortable* with waiting and wishing. And hoping. We allow ourselves to live in a state of waiting for so long, waiting becomes almost like an old friend.

The solution, which is to actually do something about the situation, is unknown—and, like everything unknown, it's scary. Doing nothing is the devil we know. Taking a chance is the devil we don't know.

We tuck ourselves in bed at night with the devil we know in fear of the devil we don't know, even if the devil we don't know yet might turn out to be a prince. If things are ever going to change, it's up to *us* to make them change.

It's up to *you*.

Branden's Magical Maxim #2
for Manifesting a Fairytale Life:

Accept total responsibility for every damn aspect of your life.

#OUATB

From the moment I opened myself up and agreed to let the universe show me what was possible, things started to happen, and they started to happen fast.

As I mentioned earlier, I'd been writing but receiving nothing but rejection after rejection. But then, out of nowhere, *I got a yes.*

I had submitted a short story to a publisher in Chicago, and they liked it enough to invite me to come to their offices to meet with them. Oh, my God, it's happening. Someone is interested in my writing. *It's finally happening!*

Then my world came crashing down.

The amazing, long-awaited *"yes"* I'd sought so relentlessly for was followed by the most devastating *"no"* imaginable—and from the last place I ever thought it would come from.

My husband.

Yes. My husband and supposed *partner* in life at the time pulled the rug out from under my dreams. He flat out told me I couldn't go.

This was someone I had given over 12 years of my life to (off and on anyway) and had shown nothing but dedication in every imaginable way, and now in my greatest moment of potential triumph—within inches of getting what I wanted and had worked so hard for—had just told me no.

"Wait—what? What do you mean I can't go?" I stammered in disbelief.

What part of no don't you get? he asked. And he wasn't done. His devastating denial of my dream was followed by an ultimatum: I could be a writer or I could be his wife.

For most of my life, I'd played small, never dialing in to me and how fucking great I could be. My mother's voice—the one I'd heard my entire childhood—rang loudly in my head. But now there was the other voice, the one that kept telling me there was more. *"It's your choice, Branden,"* he said. *"What's it going to be?"*

So this is how it happens, I thought—the moment in a person's life when the gauntlet is thrown down, and you find out what you're truly made of.

The Moment of Decision

The shock of the situation was wearing off and I felt a certain feeling of calm wash over me. No, not just calm—I felt a sense of unexpected *strength*. And *resolve*. And *acceptance*.

In our time together, I'd given my husband more love then I'd ever even given myself, and what had I gotten in return? Love? Affection? No. I got an ultimatum.

In so many ways, he was such an asshole and usually wrong about everything. But he sure as fuck was right this time. There was a choice to be made.

You bet your sweet ass there is.

I don't know exactly where the strength came from. God? The universe? Or maybe it was from the part of me that had been saying *there is more* for so long, it was a permanent part of me now. I'm not sure, perhaps it was all three. But I knew it was true. There *was* more.

I was sure of it.

I also knew the fairytale life I *really* wanted sure in the fuck wasn't going to just happen. *I had to choose it.* If I was going to find out what *more* was, it was going to be up to me and me alone.

So I decided.

I told him I would rather be single with four kids than live another minute with him not being who I wanted to be. I had goals, I told him. Dreams that won't be denied. *"The kids and I are leaving,"* I heard myself say.

He thought it was a bluff. At least until he saw me packing up the truck. Then he started back-peddling. Apologizing. But it was too late. I may have still been packing up the truck, but I was already gone.

I often think of my previous life as being overwhelmed by a gigantic wave. Suffocating. Drowning. Every time I got my head above water, another wave would hit. I'd take a gasp of air and go back under, pushed down deeper into the darkness of the ocean again and again.

Then, one day, I said fuck it. I decided to save my damn self and walked out of the water. Up onto the beach, the kids in my arms, letting the bright sunshine heat my skin, with gentle waves lapping at my ankles. I cried tears of joy, because I'd made it out. I was free. The future was waiting for me, there on the horizon.

And I was ready.

On Our Own

With little hope and even less money, I moved into a tiny two-bedroom apartment with four babies, and I wish I could tell you it was easy after that. It wasn't. If the universe was showing me the way, it was taking the long damn way around. There was no instant *happily ever after* going on, I can fucking tell you that.

My two oldest girls had to endure our devastating situation. My youngest boys were pulled away every other weekend to spend time with their father, not understanding why they couldn't live with their mother *and* father in one house.

It was a fucking mess.

But it was *my* mess.

I was writing *my* life story now, even if I had no idea of how it was going to end. But *however* it ended, it was *my* story to write.

Nobody was going to tell me I couldn't.

Not ever.

Once I finally took control of my life and got my head out of my ass, things started to change. All that bullshit waiting for a prince to come riding in on a multi-colored unicorn to save me was exactly that—*it was bullshit*—bullshit that wasn't serving me in any fucking way. But once I accepted responsibility for every damn thing in my life, everything changed. Accepting responsibility put me in control.

Is That a White Horse?

The thing that happened next was nothing short of a miracle.

Six weeks after being given the ultimatum and making the decision to leave the guy I'd thought was my prince, the man I am married to today—my *true* prince—showed up in my life. *Six weeks, bitches.*

Did I *know* he was my perfect prince right away? No. It didn't start out that way.

Truth be told, my "prince" was a crazy-selfish single guy when we met. Red flags everywhere. But—even though I'd just left a relationship—and even though I had finally decided that I didn't need to be "saved" anymore by anyone but me, we moved fast, and I jumped in with both boobs.

Wait, I know what you're thinking: It was nothing more than a rebound relationship, that I hooked up with him purely out of fear of being a single mom with four kids, forever. No shit, Sherlock. Of course it was.

But before you pass judgement, let me tell you a little bit about him.

About My Prince

I find myself hitched to the only man in the world who finds true happiness letting me live free, letting me be me— encouraging me to not only be me but to *be more of me* than I ever thought possible.

He not only gives me permission to be myself, he encourages me to be *more,* pushing me over the edge of my fears and to grab life by the balls.

What guy is secure enough to do that?

My prince charming, that's who. Yes, prince charmings like this one, they are few and far between—but trust me, they do exist. They might be hiding behind a unicorn, but they *are* out there.

We added two to the crew, and I have to say we are pretty fucking happy—not because it is the perfect fairytale life, *but because it is ours.* Differences and disagreements are things we use to grow closer. We are happy because we *choose* happiness.

We choose the laughter, we choose to dream, and, more than that, we choose love. Love for each other and these beautiful babies.

My husband is the first person in my entire life that saw *me.* He was instantly more than a lover—he was a friend. When he moved in, after four weeks of dating, my divorce wasn't even in the court system yet.

(Side note, bitches: Nothing brings an ex-husband to his knees with regret-texts begging you to come back like a new, tatted-up, hunky guy).

Quick Reality Check

While my husband is a stud, and I pride myself on making his life a little easier every day (lest you think everything in my life is really like a fairytale, chock-full of butlers and magical unicorns and other-such shit, rest assured, it's not.)

You want to know what my day-to-day reality looks like?

Okay, places, everyone…

Cue the screaming kids, fighting teens, barking dogs, hissing cats. OMG, did the baby just shit on my leg? (Yes, I now have a sixth, in case you lost count.) Yep, that's poop, definitely poop. Can someone help here, I just need a… ugh, it's on the fucking carpet now. Will someone please put the dogs outside? Zaden put some clothes on! Zaden! Boys, seriously, stop fighting over the game. Did I just step in pee? Is that pee or water? Clue: It's yellow. Is dad home yet? OMG, what time is it? Welcome to the Branden show, fuckers!

BTW: The above description *is* literally the last few minutes of my life as I was working on this chapter. Seriously. *And I love it.* How could anyone love such chaos? Because it's *my* chaos—not someone else's chaos, *but mine.* Not something forced on me. *I chose it.*

So, about those tattoos. See those tattoos on the cover of this book? *Yes, those are real,* not something airbrushed on for dramatic effect (and the rest of me is real, too, just in case you're wondering).

Admittedly, by some people's standards, I have a lot of tattoos. And if you're like most people, you're probably wondering: *What's up with that, Branden? Why all the ink?*

There are two reasons:

1. *Once I started, I simply couldn't stop.*

2. *Because I fucking like them.*

Yes, I'm a bit of a rebel, in case you hadn't figured that out yet. But there's another reason: You see, I wasn't *allowed* to have tattoos in my previous marriage. But my new best friend—the guy who outbid the universe because he wanted to hold my hand forever—said that if I wanted tattoos, I should go for it. He's not only encouraging but he's excited for me.

He loves them—because he loves me for me. I found someone who not only accepts me for me, he totally embraces the potty-mouth, attention-demanding whore I am.

(Note: My publisher insists I mention here *that my results are not a guarantee—your results may vary.*)

Okay, Full Disclosure:

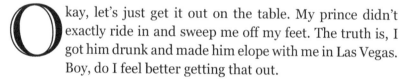

Okay, let's just get it out on the table. My prince didn't exactly ride in and sweep me off my feet. The truth is, I got him drunk and made him elope with me in Las Vegas. Boy, do I feel better getting that out.

Eight years later he still looks like a deer in headlights, but I got it done. The dude is mine. And regardless of the way we got started—rebound relationship, too many mar-tun-ies, whatever—after an ugly divorce and a custody arrangement that would break any mother's heart (no mom wants to be away from their kids for any amount of time), we are indeed living *happily ever after.*

And I doubt that anyone will ever love and adore the real me the way he does.

So how'd I get so lucky? I didn't. It wasn't luck. I made it happen. *Me.*

At a minimum, I created the conditions in which it had the possibility of happening. Because it would never have happened—never have had a *chance* of happening—had I not left my ex.

Nature Abhors a Vacuum

By saying *adios* to the man who'd refused to be a fifty-fifty partner in our relationship and support my goals and dreams as well as his own, I created what science calls *a vacuum*—not the *Hoover*-kind, of course, but the *science*-kind: a space, an emptiness, a void. (Who says you'll never use the stuff you learned in school?)

Until I'd left, with my life as crazy as it was, engulphed in the plethora of problems I'd created for myself, there was no room for solutions. No room for help. No room for a prince.

I was like one of those motels you pass on the highway at night, with my neon vacancy light burning brightly like a beacon in darkness. *I'd created a vacancy.*

I'd made *room* for a Prince Charming to arrive and from my lips to God's ear, that's *exactly* what happened.

That said, I can guarantee you this: The chances of solutions showing up for any problem you might have in your life are greatly reduced if you don't make room for them.

But if you do make room for them, you'll find that my 11th grade science teacher was right: *Nature really <u>does</u> abhor a vacuum.*

Worthy of Being Saved

It's important to realize it's not Prince Charming's job to come and save you—it's your job to be worthy of being saved. Someone who doesn't even need to be saved.

Ironic, huh?

Becoming a person who doesn't need saving—being someone capable of saving themselves—is what draws your prince into your life. And not just *a* prince, but the *right* prince. Back to Cinderella.

If there ever was a strong-ass bitch who didn't need saving, it was Cinderella. Yes, her circumstances sucked. And if it were me in that situation, I might have tossed that evil-ass stepmother in the fucking fire (and the whiny-ass sisters, too). But she's a better person than I am. Better than most of us.

Cinderella not only took their shit, she did it with grace and remained kind to others in spite of the daily cruelty being dished on her. Maybe that's why she got saved, huh?

Because even though she clearly was a victim, she never acted like one. She kept her chiseled little chin held high. She didn't beg to be saved. She was simply someone who was worthy of being saved.

Mirrors Are Magical

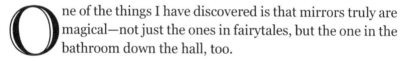 One of the things I have discovered is that mirrors truly are magical—not just the ones in fairytales, but the one in the bathroom down the hall, too.

Over the years, I have found my bathroom mirror to be a wonderful place to confront myself and get clarity on a situation. Any situation.

So, one day I did something I'd been avoiding my entire life. I stepped up to the mirror and asked:

> *Mirror, mirror, on the wall,*
> *who's the most fucked-up of all?*

Sadly, the reflection looking back at me said the thing I least wanted to hear. The mirror spoke the truth—the fucked-up person was *me*.

They say the truth shall set you free. This is true. But first the truth is really going to piss you off. The truth was, I *was* fucked-up.

That I was fucked-up inside wasn't really the revelation I'm making it out to be—it was something I'd known inwardly all along. But I'd buried it so deeply, I simply didn't want to face it. Eventually I did.

Stop Blaming Others

Not accepting responsibility lets us blame someone or something else for our miserable existence. And if we *do* take action and things don't work out, it's someone else's fault, not ours. It's *their* fault. It is the rare person who accepts 100 percent responsibility for the place they find themselves and for the decisions they made that put them there.

That's what we're avoiding. We're paralyzed with the fear of having to take responsibility.

Welcome to life, bitches.

Welcome to becoming a full-fledged adult with a bright future.

How do I know this? Because for much of my life, this was *my* story. But not anymore. Today I'm all about responsibility, motherfucker.

Now, I'd be lying if I said my dream of having a loving, caring mother is completely gone. It's still there, lingering in the recesses of my mind like a shadow. And the secret inner hope of receiving her love will probably always be with me to some degree. How could it not? I'm human.

But I no longer spend a single minute postponing my life, blaming her for her limitations and waiting for her to be what she simply isn't capable of. Instead, I've chosen to be what *I* am capable of being and have taken responsibility for my future.

If you want a fairytale life, you have to admit the things you've screwed up on and that you're not proud of, then put in the work to change it.

Take Responsibility for *Everything*

If you're going to blame anyone for the shit that happened to you, blame yourself—even if it wasn't your fault. That's what the bigger person does. And, if you prefer the word responsibility over the word blame, that's cool. Same thing as far as the universe is concerned.

Blaming yourself for your contribution to a specific event or for your circumstances in general doesn't mean you have to hate yourself for it. It just means that:

A. You're willing to admit that you may have played a part in what happened, however small.

B. There is no B.

Taking responsibility does not mean you are a bad person—to the contrary, it makes you one of those rare fabulous bitches with big enough shoulders to take the blame and maintain the posture of a queen.

Big shoulders. Chin up, carry your part of the load.

Taking responsibility lets you look at what happened, see it for what it was, and then not do it again. Admit that you played a role and that maybe you fucked up a bit.

- *You took the wrong job.*

- *Said yes when you should have said no.*

- *Married the wrong guy.*

- *Ate the fucking dessert when you promised yourself you wouldn't, rather than blaming the waiter at Cheesecake Factory.*

Want to change your future? Hold yourself accountable for your choices and actions without judging yourself. *This* is your ticket to a better future and enormous happiness.

Branden's Magical Maxim #3
for Manifesting a Fairytale Life:

Stop comparing yourself to others and just fucking be you.

#OUATB

I want to start this section by helping you face the truth about something—something you may not even realize. And that truth is that you have a sickness. *You have a disease. (Thanks Branden, I was actually starting to feel good about myself, and now you hit me with this?)*

The disease I'm referring to is:

Comparititis.

You're not the only person who has it. We all have it, including yours truly. I get caught up in playing the comparison game, too, sometimes.

Living our lives by comparison is a really fucked-up part of our DNA, a bullshit illness where we measure ourselves against what other people have *(that we don't)*, the way they look *(and we don't)*, and what they've achieved *(that we haven't)*.

Girls tend to do it with ring size.

Guys do it with their dicks.

Nothing kills happiness and contentment more quickly than comparing ourselves to others. I am not overstating this: It is a fucking disease that sucks the joy from our souls. Even worse, it's virtually impossible *not* to get infected by it (well, maybe there's an enlightened Gandhi-like monk sitting on the top of a mountain in India somewhere without WIFI who doesn't suffer from it but aside from that exception, we *all* suffer).

Today, the disease has turned into a widespread epidemic because of social media, which has blown the problem up to massive fucking proportions like nothing we've ever experienced before.

Too many people allow their self-esteem and self-worth to be tied up by their social media status. If no one "likes" you, does that mean you're unlikable? No.

Always Someone "Better"

For years, people used to try to *"keep up with the Joneses."* Now we've moved up a letter in the alphabet, from the *Joneses* to the *Kardashians.*

If you look for ways to be unhappy by comparing yourself to others, you're going to find there are always the Joneses or Kardashians out there somewhere. Spend five minutes on Instagram or Facebook and you will find someone who is better than you at something, thinner and/or healthier than you are, richer than you are, with a bigger castle than you have, and/or is prettier than you in some way (unless you ask my husband, since he has been fully trained to say there is no one in the universe prettier than I am!)

Newsflash, bitches: *What you see on Instagram and Facebook isn't real*—it's someone's *airbrushed versions* of reality. God, it's bad enough that we tend to compare ourselves to others. Now we spend our time comparing ourselves to what other's *pretend to be* and *pretend to have.* People are rarely the things they post.

Fucking stop it, already! *Okay?*

The pursuit of perfection is simply the fear of not being good enough compared to others. So stop that shit. Just work on being good enough for you.

Stop trying to be Kylie, Kendall or (fill in the blank with the "influencer" of your choice). You want to admire them? Fine. You want to emulate some of the things they've achieved? I say, go for it. But stop wasting your time trying to *be* them.

I've learned to ignore the pictures people post on Instagram and on their Facebook page (unless what they're sharing is themselves at their worst, in which case I not only look at it, I gawk at it—and applaud it).

Oscar Wilde is quoted as having said: *"Be yourself, everyone else is taken."* I say, *"Be yourself, everyone else can fuck off."*

Your gifts are your gifts and are like no one else's in the world. But no one will ever know that as long as you keep comparing and using that comparison to stay stuck.

Being Perfectly Imperfect

In so many ways I am a hot mess. The mom pulling up in the pick-up lane, bumping to Snoop Dog, in three-day old sweats, breast-milk drenched hoody, a child who looks feral, a crying, poopy baby, and boys with disheveled hair—always pushing for time, that's me. I am unorganized and chaotic and I hate cleaning house.

I have zero housekeeping skills. Nor do I have a desire to attain them. When I say our house is chaos, it's an understatement. It's a cluster fuck of things I keep promising to deal with later.

My husband is a lucky fucker because I am perfect. I only fuck up all of the time, and I know I am high maintenance. No apologies. I like what I like, and I want what I want. And the sooner he gets on board, the happier we all are. Truly, bitches, pray for my husband. He had no idea what he was getting himself into by marrying me.

Now, I can focus on my flaws all day long if I want to. Or, if I choose, I can focus on my strengths. I can spend my time telling myself how fat I am, or how I fucked my makeup up before heading out. Or I can focus on the fact that I'm an amazing mentor. Great leader. Good friend. Hell of a writer. And I love hard, sometimes for no reason at all, deserving or undeserving, whether I know you or not, just because I think you are fucking awesome. Or have the potential to be.

It's okay to be a hot mess. You don't have to be PTA Pam or Dr. Phil perfect (if that's your definition of perfection) to be awesome in your own way. Or many ways. Stop with the fucking comparison bullshit, okay? And stop using your perceived imperfections as excuses to stay stuck. Embrace the kick-ass bitch you *are*, not the person you *think* you're supposed to be, and do this damn thing.

No one out there has their shit together completely. No one has the perfect life, and no one makes the perfect decisions. Your goal should be to find the balance that works for you, and then fuck everybody else.

Haters Gonna Hate

I don't even know where to start with the issue of haters. I can't count how many times I have been told to go kill myself on social media. I've been called names I forget and even had my kids attacked verbally. The internet has opened the floodgates to an ocean of trolls, people who are unhappy with who they are, unhappy with their lives, and do everything within their power to make other people feel as small and shitty as they do.

Is some of the crazy stuff I say, write and believe *eye-roll* worthy? *Sure it is.* Have I been accused of being "extra?" *You bet your ass (and mine) I have.*

Do I care? *Hell no.*

I went through a period where I hated the haters, only to realize that I was lowering myself to their level. Now I do everything within my power to show them love and kindness. It's not fucking easy, but I try. But don't you dare fuck with my kids. You come after my kids, and I will track you down and cut your (insert body part of your choice) off.

I wish children growing up in this generation could somehow understand that people say the vilest of things to them and about them because *they* are so damaged inside and because they feel the only way to rise up is to pull someone else down. But when you're young, it's a hard thing to get.

Today's kids have it so much worse. Teen suicide rates are up because bullying is relentless and staying anonymous is way too easy. At least when I was growing up, I knew who was talking smack about me and could go kick their ass if I felt like it.

Trolls Shouldn't Dull Your Shine

Whenever I encounter anything written by a hate-tossing troll, here's what I do: I read what they've written in a ridiculously slow, over exaggerated voice, until the words lose their sharp edges and I start to laugh. Then I spend the next few seconds in gratitude and being thankful that I am nothing like them.

I wish I could say it's easy to go through life and not care what others think, but the truth is we all care. You just can't let a hater's sentiments dull your shine.

If it was even worth the energy, I would say you should feel sorry for them, but they aren't worth the time.

There is something positive to being trolled, though. Really, there is. It's that having to learn to deal with them makes for thick skin. And thick skin is a requirement for success. And happiness.

If you choose to be in the public eye on any sort of platform (like I have), you *will* be attacked.

You *will* be judged.

A lot. And harshly.

You've got to learn to deal, bitch. And when you do, the trolls may have accidently become an indispensable part of your ultimate success.

Defining Success

Success is different for everyone, clearly. Right now, with an 8-month-old baby in my arms as I type this, I define success as getting clothes onto both of us.

Success doesn't have anything to do with your bank account, either. So don't think you can't speak up in a meeting or approach someone with a business idea just because you think they're "more successful" than you are. Fantastic Fran may be making $1 million per year and you've only got only $47.22 in the bank.

Your idea could be worth $10 million, maybe more, who knows? You'll never know unless you speak up and take a chance.

Success also has nothing to do with followers, likes or clicks. And it sure as fuck isn't about approval from friends and family.

Move the fuck on with that shit.

"Success" is what *you* say it is. It is waking up ☺AF to be alive. Success is wearing your heart on the outside and sharing a gift with another human. Success is happiness in the things you *do*, not in the things you *have*.

Success isn't ANYTHING anyone else tells you it is. It's what you tell yourself it is. Which ultimately means that, if you're taking my advice, you should ignore everything I just said success is and/or isn't because, in the end, only *you* can define what in the fuck success is for you. Only you.

Only you.

Don't let me or anyone else define what makes you happy. Your inner feelings define what success is, and your smile describes it to the world.

Fran thinks I am a hot mess, and she's right. Karen thinks I'm a superstar, and she's right, too. Neither of their opinions affect my definition. Neither of their judgements dulls my shine.

I know I'm a success because I have everything I've ever wanted, saggy boobs and all. I could do without some of the cellulite, but now we're just nitpicking.

Becoming Self-Aware

Defining success for yourself requires a certain amount of self-awareness. This is a double-edged sword, a painful process for some. You have to dig deep to remember who you are and what you really wanted before the world began imprinting its marketing messages on you and planting its fucked-up seeds of desire inside of your subconscious.

For example, the amount of money projected to be spent on advertising in the United States in 2019 is almost $200 billion dollars, much of which is directed at children (evil fuckers). So by the time you're an adult, you barely remember what it was that you really wanted anymore—your true wants and desires have been bombarded with ads and buried in bullshit.

You have to be aware of who you are—what *your* thoughts are, not the media's; what *your* likes and dislikes are, not *your* neighbors or co-workers—and then showing up confidently in the pursuit of those things.

Being self-aware requires defining what *your* true fairytale life would look like to you, not to someone else.

It's being in touch with your truest values and deepest-held beliefs. It's turning on a flashlight and shining it on your *real* goals and desires—*not what others think your goals and desires should be.*

Once you get through the wants and desires that have been planted there by other people, then and only then can you come into your own.

Ask "Why?" Before You Buy

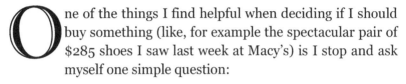 ne of the things I find helpful when deciding if I should buy something (like, for example the spectacular pair of $285 shoes I saw last week at Macy's) is I stop and ask myself one simple question:

Why do I want them?

The quick and easy answer is, *because I want them.* Which is always true. But then I'll ask myself:

Yes, I know that, but why?

To which the voice in my head usually responds with, *"I already told you, I want them because I want them."* So then I'll say to myself:

Come on, Branden, answer the question:
Why do you REALLY want them?

And it is usually at this point where the truth emerges, which is: *I want them to impress people.*

I don't really need these shoes at all. I've got 14 pairs of really great shoes in the closet already. The only reason I want these shoes is because of the reaction I'm going to get from Snarky Susan, who is always showing off the latest fashions. Oh, my God, I'm not buying them for myself at all! I want them to impress Susan!

The truth hurts. But the truth is the truth, and it just saved me $285 I could use for back-to-school clothes for the kids, surprise my husband with tickets to the game he wants to go to (shitty seats, probably, but so what, it's the thought), and/or buy a hundred other things we really need.

Slow Yourself Down

When I learned to slow myself down, I realized that most of what I spent money on were things I didn't really need and only made me happy for a few days, two weeks, tops. And I was buying them for entirely the wrong reason. I was buying shit to impress friends, colleagues and (even worse) fucking strangers.

Strangers!

It's in these moments of truth we see just how much of our time, money and mental energy is spent trying to make ourselves happy and going about it the wrong way.

Quit trying to impress others. Shoes and jewelry are not the only way to happiness. For that matter, screw happiness—*go for joy, instead.*

- *Joy is freedom.*
- *Joy is discipline.*
- *Joy is chasing your dream, even if you fall short.*
- *Joy is being a real role model for your kids.*
- *Joy is dying without regrets.*

And sometimes the best path to joy is to tell yourself *no.*

Then, when you walk into work next week and see that snarky, boney-ass bitch, you can look at her, smile and know you won the competition—*because you refused to play.*

Don't misunderstand what I've been saying. I'm not saying you shouldn't treat yourself to stuff—if I was, it would make me one big-ass hypocrite. I've got a closet jammed with things I've treated myself to! I'm only suggesting you pause and ask yourself, *why?*

Wanting things is normal. It's good to want things. But you should want the things you want because *you* really want them because they make *you* happy, not simply to impress some stranger. For example, I love feeling glamorous. Mom life is the *opposite* of glamorous.

A Defining Moment

One of my defining moments as a mom was a day when I woke late to get the kids ready for school and snapped at everyone rather than taking responsibility for myself. I became self-aware of how my behavior was affecting others and realized that I was always happier when I woke up earlier, early enough to throw on some makeup. Which happens to be one of my superpowers.

I don't know what it is about some contouring that makes me feel like the royal bitch I am. I *love* feeling glamorous, and I'm proud to admit it.

It's not ideal to change diapers in high heels and red lipstick with my hair a foot tall, but you better believe I enjoy every moment when I get to do it.

In my fairytale life, there's a glam squad around the corner to help me face every day like the queen I am without me having to do the work. But baby cuddles are a hard thing to give up just to have a fancy hairdo. In my dream world—in *my* fairytale—I get both.

I do everything in my power to give myself time to put on my makeup because I want what I want. But here's the key: I want what I want for me. *Not for anyone else. No one else's involvement is required.* I never do it for others (unless I'm doing a Facebook live or something, which is ultimately for me, anyway). I'll also spend thirty minutes doing my makeup sometimes even if I'm not going to see a soul.

You Are Enough Already

Don't travel down the road of trying to be liked by everyone else. Everything you are right now is fucking royalty. You are enough just the way you are.

And when you do see the things that other people have, finding yourself devolving into negative thoughts of comparison, dig deep inside yourself and, rather than coming up with a hand clenched with jealousy and envy, be happy for them. Celebrate their good fortune.

Show gratitude to the universe for delivering the person such wealth and abundance. As the saying goes: *Hating those who have is not the way to become one of them.*

Know that you are enough already.

- *You are fucking awesome enough already to achieve virtually any goal you set your mind to.*

- *You are beautiful enough already to have virtually any prince you want.*

- *You are smart enough to achieve virtually any goal.*

There is no one exactly like you in the world with your talents, abilities and gifts. No one.

So stop fucking looking outside yourself. Quit trying to *compete*. Quit trying to *be* someone else. Accept your imperfections and know that you are fucking amazing in your own right. *I know that I am* (just this moment I got a whiff of the diaper I didn't throw out three hours ago, and even with that said, I know that I am enough). *Because I am me.*

Now, just start being you.

Branden's Magical Maxim #4
for Manifesting a Fairytale Life:

Dream dreams that are so big they make people doubt you.

#OUATB

H ello, my name is Branden, and I'm a compulsive dreamer."

DREAMER'S ANONYMOUS LEADER: *"What's your date, Branden?*

ME: *"My what?"*

D.A. LEADER: *"Your date. When did your compulsive dreams start?"*

ME: *"Start? Uh, they didn't. They just always were."*

My dreams have always been there, always been with me. I can remember no inciting incident where suddenly my dreams were kindled. They have simply been there, like standard options on a car.

And I'm pretty sure I'm not alone. Chances are good, since you are reading this book, that you and I are the same. We both have fantasies of living the good life. We both want to do great things with our lives. The ranks of the dreamers out there are legion.

Everything starts with a dream.

In my case, I am a crazy dreamer. Once I reach one goal, I find 10 more that are bigger and better. Average is never enough for me.

The truth is, my dreams are far past any idea of what's normal. I know that. But they're my dreams, and nobody can tell me I can't have them. And I push for them constantly.

I am in perpetual action.

My goals are more important to me than water.

I've already told you about my primary dreams: happy hubby, healthy children (if they're happy, that's a bonus), building my work-from-home business, and becoming a successful best-selling author. Oh, and a speaker. And developing my coaching business.

And...and...and...

If I told you all the things that were on my dream list, you'd think I was nuts. I give birth to dreams almost as fast as I give birth to children.

Kids Dream Big

Ever ask a child what they want to be when they grow up? The answers are cute, aren't they? The kid says, *"I want to be an astronaut!"*

We smile. And nod. And respond with something like, *"Oh that's great!"* While inside we're secretly thinking: *"No fucking way, kid. Do you have any idea how fucking hard it is to be an astronaut? NASA takes like 20 people a year, and they're all math and science geeks. You'll be lucky to get to Cleveland."*

Well, you know what? That's exactly what I want people to think when I tell them my dreams. I *want* them to doubt me. No, I want them to think I'm a fucking crazy dreamer. I thrive on their doubt. I've learned to enjoy it.

Your dreams should be so big that everyone doubts you when *you* share them, too.

In any case, your dreams should be **big.**

Wait, that's not big enough (where in the hell is the 36 pt. *Haettenschweiler* font when you need it?) Ah, here it is...

No, no, no.

I'm talking really, really...

"**B**" for "bold."

"**I**" for "incomprehensible."

"**G**" for "glorious."

Better.

Your dreams should be *bold* enough to inspire you to take action... *incomprehensible* at the time you set them as to how you're going to achieve them...and *glorious* enough that when you *do* achieve them, everyone says, *"She did what? You're fucking kidding me. I had no idea she had it in her."*

For most people, the quickest way to kill a big dream is to share it with a small-minded person.

If you can't let the doubts of others roll off you, then don't share them.

The choice is yours: Ignore the opinions of others—but, if you can't—keep your dreams to yourself.

Beware of "Dream Stealers"

Fact: The world is filled with dream stealers. It took me a while to learn this, but I know it now. They're out there, lurking in the night, just waiting to snatch them away from you.

Many of the people who will sabotage your dreams will do so in the name of friendship. They're not your friends. Others are family members who claim to love you, who *"only want the best for you."*

For everything I've done in my life that got me where I am, to my current state of happiness, there were five people who told me I shouldn't.

You try to explain to them what you want and why you want it. But they don't get it. And why? Because the dreams are yours, they're not theirs. It's not their fault for not understanding—the dreams you have weren't given to them—they were given to you.

Tell enough people, and there will always be someone who will point out something negative—a reason why your plan won't work. Don't give them the power.

This is something that I wish I had known sooner and could implant in my kids, instead of them learning the hard way. I work on telling them this every day. And now I'm telling you.

Ignore everyone and just do your thing.

And, by the way, the next time you doubt the dreams of a child, realize what you're really doing. What you're *really* doing is doubting *your* ability to achieve *your* dreams. Because if you knew you could achieve any dream you set your mind to, you wouldn't doubt theirs.

Perfect Circumstances Be Damned

Sometimes my dreams conflict with the needs of my family. I need my sanctuary to let my mind create as it was meant to, which doesn't always match up with my husband's schedule. While he is sound asleep at 8:30 each night, I'm blasting some random BoJack Horseman on Netflix and knocking out word count in bed, wedged between a sleeping baby and cranky toddler. When he wakes up, as the sun starts peaking over the horizon, I am closing my laptop and finally falling asleep.

Dreams don't require perfect circumstances to be achieved. And as one of my mentors, John Maxwell, said: "Dreams don't work unless you do."

I don't complain. I just do the work.

And I don't throw in the towel when things get tough. If I did, I'd be throwing it in a hundred times per day.

"But you don't understand, Branden—I've got to work. I've got bills to pay. I've got a family. I've got obligations. I've got to volunteer for the bake sale at my daughter's school on Saturday. My back is out. My car is in the shop. Someone stole my laptop. My boss wants me to work the weekend. I've got this, I've got that. I'm stuck!"

Stuck? What do you mean, you're stuck? *You're not a fucking tree.* Your roots aren't planted, bitch—unless you want them to be. Take responsibility for where you are. Be mindful that it was all a choice, and if you don't like it, this is your do over.

Move your bitch ass, damnit!

No Excuses

If you think you were going to get to this point of the book and I was going to start cutting you slack, you haven't been paying attention. Maybe that "I can't do it" bullshit works on other people in your life. It doesn't work on me. I've been through too much and come through it to accept bullshit excuses.

There are no excuses.

- *Yes, there are things that will delay your dreams...*

- *There will be the occasional road closure/unavoidable detour that may force you to take a different route...*

- *There will be floods and hurricanes and power outages and a hundred other things guaranteed to get in your way...*

So fucking what? Those things are just excuses. If you know what you want and want it badly enough, small shit (and that's what we've been talking about here: small shit) never gets in the way.

The Power of Vision Boards

Oh, God, Branden, you're not going to talk about vision boards, are you?" Fucking right, I am. Why? Because they're important, and because they work.

But before I launch into the reasons you must have a vision board (and how to build one), let me take a quick moment to explain what a vision board is.

A vision board (also referred to as dream boards) are basically a collection of words and pictures that represent the goals and dreams you want to achieve.

The reason you must have one (or many) is because they're the most effective tool you can use to imprint your goals and dreams on your mind.

For example, my vision board has had pictures of books on them for as long as I can remember.

And now I'm writing one.

As Jack Canfield, co-author of the "Chicken Soup for the Soul"® series and "The Success Principles," and one of the most brilliant men to ever walk the planet, describes them this way:

> *"Your brain will work tirelessly to achieve the statements you give your subconscious mind. And when those statements are the affirmations and images of your goals, you are destined to achieve them!"*
>
> *– Jack Canfield*

Having dreams is important. Making those dreams visual is critical. Because vision boards are literally "snapshots of your future." I'd go so far as to say:

> *Show me your vision board, and I'll show you your future.*

Celebrities Use Them, Too

Still not sold on having a vision board? I've already explained that Jack Canfield, who has sold half a billion books, believes in them. Is he alone? No. You know who else used vision boards to fuel their success? Ellen DeGeneres. Katy Perry. Oprah. And Kellan Lutz (from the *Twilight* saga) had one, too. Steve Harvey swears by them. And the story about Jim Carrey is fucking crazy.

In the early 1990s, Jim Carrey was a penniless unknown, doing his best to merely survive. For motivation, he wrote himself a check for

$10 million for "acting services rendered" and post-dated it for 1994.

He carried that check in his wallet for four years. Looking at it every day.

At night, Jim Carrey would park his car on Mulholland Drive and gaze down at the valley lights, visualizing his success. Four years later, he signed a deal for the lead role in the movie "Dumb and Dumber"...

For $10 million dollars.

(insert chills here)

Jim Carrey's vision board measured just 2.5 by 6 inches, proving once and for all that size doesn't matter—*it's all in how you use it.*

Are you listening, guys?

Repetitive Visualization

That's right. Merely creating a vision board doesn't mean shit. You've got to *use it.* You've got to *visualize* and *internalize* your goals and dreams every damn day. Actually, twice a day is better.

I sit in front of my vision board for 10 minutes every morning and visualize my dreams. I also do this when I wake up and at night, right before I go to sleep (hence the term dream board). And when you do your visualization, you visualize your goals and dreams as if they have already come true.

Can you spell *Law of Attraction?*

Albert Einstein once said, *"Imagination is everything. It's the preview to life's coming attractions."* We're talking Einstein, bitches. Motherfucking Einstein!

There is so much research out there validating how visualization activates your subconscious mind. And if you're *still* not sold on how important imagination and visualization are, the only thing I can do is ask: *So, how is not visualizing the fairytale life you want working out for you so far?*

Make no mistake—vision boards are some powerful shit and not to be taken lightly. The things you cut out and paste on your board, and focus on intensely and consistently, are *going* to come about. Trust me, *they are.* Maybe not, today, or even tomorrow—*but eventually.*

So don't fuck around.

Take the process seriously.

Only include the things you really want. No, not just want, but *crave*—things that will truly make you happy, not unimportant shit. What qualifies as unimportant shit? Stuff like Birkin bags, yachts, and Lamborghinis. God, if I see one more YouTube video with someone standing in front of a (probably rented) Lambo, trying to convince themselves they're happy, I'm going to throw up in my mouth.

Fuck that shit.

That's not what's going to make you happy. And if it does, the happiness is only going to be temporary. So don't clutter your vision board with that crap, okay? Because if you do, it's only going to dilute your focus and reduce your chances of getting the things that really matter to you.

For me, the things that matter include happy, healthy children, a happy, healthy husband, and a happy, healthy Branden, not necessarily in that order.

Everything else is superfluous.

Everything else is *nice* to have, not *got* to have.

The Original 'Pretty Woman' Ending

So, if vision boards are so damn powerful, why doesn't everyone have one? The answer, I believe, is contained in the original screenplay for "Pretty Woman."

Wait, didn't we talk about "Pretty Woman" already? Yes, but there's something really interesting I didn't tell you earlier.

The original screenplay, by writer J.F. Lawton (titled "3,000", which related to the $3,000 Edward pays Vivian to spend the week with him), was a much darker story about the perils of prostitution, the dangers of drugs, and capitalistic greed.

No wonder they changed it, right?

No one wants to see that shit.

So it was altered by a studio honcho (who, by chance, just happened to be a woman!) who told the director to turn it into something that would make people feel good—you know, like a fairytale. The result was the movie we know today, one of Hollywood's most successful and deeply loved films of all time.

But in the original screenplay, Vivian and Edward don't end up together. That's right. *He didn't go to her apartment and save her.* Even worse, the original screenplay ended on a decidedly down note, with Vivian and her roommate, Kit, on a bus bound for Disneyland (aka, "The Happiest Place on Earth"), staring blankly out the window as an endless parade of pawn shops and strip clubs pass by.

Vivian isn't saved.

She's abandoned.

And devastated.

The Dream Is Over

Not only doesn't Vivian get her Prince Charming, she's forced to accept that the dream is over. She is forced to return to the reality of her sad, pathetic life, the message being: *This is what happens when poor people get to see everything rich people have, especially if they've never experienced it before.* No fucking doves being released with that ending.

(This seems like the perfect time for a heavily dreadlocked, street-dwelling Rastafarian to appear and say something profound.) Let's see, how about this?

STREET-DWELLING RASTAFARIAN

Welcome to Hollywood. What's your dream?
Everybody comes here. This is Hollywood, the
land of dreams. Some dreams come true, some
don't. But keep on dreaming. This is Hollywood.
Always time to dream, so keep on dreaming.

Yes, perfect. Which leads me to my theory about why most of us stop dreaming.

Why We Stop Dreaming

I believe the reason most people stop dreaming is: *Because it's simply too fucking painful to constantly remind ourselves of the things we do not have—and, worse—the things we believe we will never get.* We're afraid that we'll end up like Vivian, sitting on a bus bound for Disneyland, staring out the window as pawn shops and strip clubs pass by.

- *We're afraid we'll never be able to quit our soul-sucking jobs so we stop dreaming about the freedom of owning our own business...*

- *We're afraid we'll never be able to lose the weight so we stop dreaming about what it would be like to be thin again...*

- *We're afraid we'll never own the Lexus so we stop dreaming about it, telling ourselves how happy we are with our piece-of-crap Toyota Corolla...*

- *We're afraid we'll never get to Paris to see the Eiffel Tower so we stop dreaming about going...*

- *We're afraid we'll never own that magnificent house from "Architectural Digest" so we tear up the picture and throw it away because it's fucking painful to see it all the time...*

Newsflash: You will never get the things you want by not looking at them. No matter how painful it is to remind yourself of what you've yet to accomplish and what you don't yet have, you've got to keep dreaming.

Always time to dream, so keep on dreaming.

Branden's Magical Maxim #5
for Manifesting a Fairytale Life:

Your life is the sum of your choices.

Choose well.

#OUATB

I used to think life was complicated. It's not. Life is simple. *We're* complicated. *We're* the ones who complicate the shit out of things. We do it to ourselves.

So, what's the solution?

Choices.

I've done my best to avoid making points by quoting other people since I assume you didn't buy this book to have me tell you what everyone *else* thinks. But—when it comes to the subject of choices—quotes seem appropriate. (Hang on while I find my trusty pocket-quote guide.) Ah, here it is...

"Make good choices."

— Anna Kendrick, from the movie "Pitch Perfect"

"Everything you are comes from your choices."

— Jeff Bezos, founder of Amazon & richest fucker in the world

"May your choices reflect your hopes, not your fears."

— Nelson Mandela/Maya Angelou/Abraham Lincoln/Oprah (take your pick, it's always one of them)

Good quotes, all of them. But none of them hold a candle to this one:

"Choices are the hinges of destiny."

— Pythagoras

Or, the modern-day update from W. Clement Stone, who said:

"Little hinges swing big doors."

Choices Are "Hinges"

You know what a *hinge* is, right? If not, look at any door in your house and see the metal-thing with the screws that's holding it on? That's a hinge.

Most doors have either two or three hinges, depending on the door's size and weight. What's amazing is that a couple of 4-inch hinges can swing a 60-pound door. Hinges...

- Can open the doors of happiness, freedom, and opportunity...*or they can close them.*

- Can open the doors to a healthy life...*or close them.*

- Can open the doors to your future...*or keep them closed.*

This is not one of those cute concepts you can just brush off and move on with your life like someone just told you to have a nice day. This concept is important. This concept is powerful. This is a big fucking deal—maybe the most important section of the book.

Don't gloss over it, bitches.

One of the problems facing us, especially today, is that we have too many choices. Two hundred years ago this problem didn't exist. Back then, people had very few choices, so making them was simpler:

- *Work in the coal mine or in the factory.*

- *Sail to freedom or stay where you are.*

- *Work the farm and eat, or don't work the farm and fucking die.*

Limited choices, but easy choices to make. Today, we have the opposite: a seemingly endless array of options that often feel overwhelming, suffocating, even paralyzing.

If you live in a first-world country in the 21st century, you live in a world of abundance. Abundance is everywhere. Even if you don't have it, you can see it. We're fucking lucky, bitches: There are places in the world where you could walk in any direction for seven days and not see a fucking goat, let alone a Cold Stone Creamery.

Every Choice Matters

Some of life's choices are clearly big ones: Who we choose to marry. Whether or not to have children. What career we should pursue. Decisions this big impact the shit out of the joy and happiness we'll experience in life.

Other choices seem small and insignificant in comparison—like which shampoo to use, or which color to paint the living room walls—and have very little to do with how life eventually turns out.

Or maybe they do.

I contend that *every* choice matters. Big choices, small choices, and in-between choices, they all matter. *Every single fucking one of them.*

They *all* matter.

Because every single choice we've ever made has helped mold us into who we are today. And every single choice we make from this moment forward will determine who we'll become tomorrow.

Take a minute and look around your house (if you're not at home, do this the minute you walk in the door). Look at every single thing you own: your TV, your sofa, your bed, the art hanging on the walls, and the books on the shelves, and the clothes hanging in your closet—and realize this:

Every single item you own, every single thing you have in your life (as well as the things you don't have in your life) are the result of past choices. Every single thing, all of it was *you*. Big choices, small choices, and everything in between, they all added up to where you are, who you are, and what you have.

It was all you.

The life you are living right now is the one *you choose* to live. You chose it. Not someone else.

No one forced it on you. You chose it. *You.*

Ouch.

Seriously. You're not happy with your life? Why? You chose it. I know what you're thinking: *This isn't the life I want.*

I get it. There were many times I wasn't living the life I wanted. But it was still the life I chose. And the same goes for you. You're not happy with it? Chose another life. You are in control.

The Next Right Thing

What I'm about to say may sound simplistic but if I were to offer one piece of advice that will make the biggest impact on your life five years from now as a result of having read this book, it's this:

> *Choose to do the "next right thing"—no matter how uncomfortable it makes you— rather than the next easy and fun thing.*

Be willing to suffer and sacrifice a bit. Be willing to postpone luxury and comfort and immediate gratification for something better and bigger and greater somewhere on down the road.

Are you willing to do that?

Are you?

I'll tell you this: If your answer is no, I predict that five years from now your life will be almost exactly like it is this very minute—or perhaps even worse. But if the answer is yes, I predict your life will be better. A lot better.

Now, to be clear, this is the current-Branden talking—*the today me*. The old me, the 10-years-ago me, would have told you the exact opposite. The old me would have told you to party, to screw that *sacrifice for tomorrow* bullshit. But the now-me knows better. The *now-me* gets it.

Are you ready to get it? Are you going to get clear on what you want and choose behaviors that track with those things? Or are you going to read these words, nod like you agree, then continue on doing the same bullshit that brought you to this place, wishing things were better?

If the you from five years ago had made better choices, you'd be exactly where you wanted to be right now. But *that you* didn't.

Now, what about *this you?*

Does *this you* love the future you enough to sacrifice a bit of temporary pleasure as a gift to the future you? Do you love yourself that much? For a long time I didn't.

I do now.

Choose Forgiveness

One of the biggest choices you will ever make is in the area of forgiveness. When it comes to the hurt and anger and rage you've been carrying inside you about any wrong you have suffered, you must find a way to forgive the person who fucked you over.

The years I spent wondering about the decisions my mom made, never being able to relate or fully understand and never getting an explanation or any form of closure was killing me. The only answer was to forgive her, especially since no apology or explanation was on the horizon.

So I've forgiven her.

Please notice I didn't say forgive and forget. I'll never be able to forget some of the fucked-up shit people have done to me—*but I've forgiven them.* You must forgive the people who have hurt you too, every last fucking one of them.

Fully.

Entirely.

Even though you'll never forget what they did to you.

Reclaim Your Power

You are never more powerful than that moment you choose to forgive someone who has done you wrong and never apologized for it. Of all the bags of fucks I have thrown away, the one filled with anger over having been done wrong, this was the hardest one to toss.

I've got other things to do with my time, like take care of my prince and my little angels. And write my book. And build my coaching business. I had their poisonous bullshit forced down my throat once already, I'm not about to drink it again.

Now, don't just nod your head, bitch. Don't blow this off. Try it. Like right now.

I'll wait.

You don't even have to do it to their face or call them. Just do it by saying aloud:

"I forgive you for _____."

Forgiveness is a remarkable *miracle drug* that is more addictive than opioids. Once you've fully forgiven someone for the wrongs they've committed (real or imagined), you'll get hooked on it.

I promise.

Let It Go, Frozen

I heard someone say that *"holding onto anger is like drinking poison and hoping the other person will die."* Or maybe it was resentment. Or was it holding onto grudges? Anyway, you get the point.

Buddha said, *"Holding on to anger is like grasping a hot coal with the intent of harming another. It's you who ends up getting burned."* Score one for Buddha.

When you hold on to *any* of the shit people have done to you, you only end up hurting yourself. You've got to let it go, bitches. *Let it go...Let it go...Let it go...* (I think I hear Idina Menzel singing in the background, damn it.)

Seriously, bitches. By holding on to the pain, you are only hurting yourself. Let go of that shit. Drop the hot coal. Pour out the poison.

But, Branden, I don't have any big, earthshattering trauma in my past to let go of, just the normal shit everyone goes through. You know, stuff like my parents wouldn't let me get a dog. I don't care. No matter how small the hurt, if you remember it 18 years later, you've got to Idina Menzel that shit.

Remember earlier when I said nature abhors a vacuum? How is the universe supposed to deliver you a sack of joy when there's no place to put it because there's no room for it?

Empty that shit out.

Create a vacuum—a space for the universe to put the joy.

Let it go.

Love and Kindness Rocks

You know what hurts people more than showing them your anger and contempt? Showing them kindness and forgiveness. That's right. If you really want to get even, show the people who hurt you that you are bigger than they are through kindness and forgiveness.

That shit will fuck someone up.

No matter how big the asshole, slay them with kindness. People who try to hurt you or sabotage your success, the people who are completely jealous of your potential, kill them with kindness. Kindness and love.

Then sit back, embrace your belief in cosmic justice and let karma handle the rest. Trust me, the universe has your back. One way or another, the thoughtlessness (and sometimes outright meanness) of others will get rubbed in their face eventually. You don't need to do it yourself. You're bigger than that. Right?

Rather than hating people for their actions, *thank them.*

Yes, I mean it: *Thank the people who wronged you.* Seriously. Thank them for the power that you now possess because you were strong enough to forgive when they weren't sorry.

Real bitches own their shit.

You are chasing the wrong rabbit down the wrong hole if you are looking for ways to make others pay for their actions. The only thing that happens is you look like an insecure dumbass. I don't know how else to put it.

There is so much more out there for you, for us all, but we have to earn it by loving others, not hating them. That's how we earn it.

Find your power.

Hold your head high.

And fuck everybody who ever hurt you not with hate, but with gratitude, a smile, a hug, and a sweet *I love you.*

Choose Gratitude

It's easy to appreciate the good stuff that happens to us in life. What's harder is to appreciate everything, including the bad.

I've come to appreciate *everything* that was handed to me in this life. Everything. I'm not only willing to forgive the people who did me wrong, I appreciate them for it. All of it.

I appreciate their ignorance.

I appreciate their lack of caring.

I even appreciate their hate.

I didn't give them the power to win. My life of gratitude and abundance is the biggest F-you to everybody who wronged me, didn't believe in me, and told me no. I'm living my life *my* way, and I love them for *their* part in it. I would not be the person I am in the present without their part in my past. I love them for what they both *did* and *didn't* do because that's part of what made me who I am. I am grateful for the love they showed me, and their hatred and bullshit, too.

All of it.

For every word of rejection, every show of lack of faith, every pound of meanness and ounce of thoughtlessness. Every damn bit of it.

Thankful.

Drown yourself in gratitude for everything that's happened to you in your life, everything you own and everything you don't, everything you are and everything you aren't, and everything to come regardless of what's coming. Good or bad. Be grateful.

Be fucking grateful for it all.

Wait? Did I just tell you to be grateful even for bad things? Yes. Why? First, because no matter how bad something is, it could always be worse. And, second, because for bad shit to happen to you, you have to be alive. And alive is always good.

Always.

Doors Open and Close

Do you believe the saying, *For every door that closes, the universe opens another one?* I do. And I believe that every time someone slammed a door in my face in the past, they unknowingly opened a door for me somewhere—that the universe used everyone else's actions *for* me, not against me, helping me become the person I was meant to be.

I believe I am an amazing mom and damn good wife *precisely* because of the things I experienced, both good and bad. Given the chance to go back and change the past, I wouldn't change a fucking thing.

I own the choices I made. I own the choices I didn't make, too. I own them all, appreciate them all, and accept them all as perfect because they made me, me.

Me.

If my kingdom is fucked up, it's because of *my* choices.

If you aren't living your fairytale life, it isn't because of some force *outside* of yourself—it's because of the forces at work *inside* of you. Your thoughts and feelings.

And your choices.

Branden's Magical Maxim #6
for Manifesting a Fairytale Life:

Eliminate everything evil and negative from your kingdom.

#OUATB

Okay, here's where I get to play badass and rachet things up a bit. Ready? It is my belief that anyone in your life who insists on polluting your garden with their never-ending toxic bullshit and unacceptable behaviors must go.

And, yes, this includes your so-called *bullshit friends and faux-family members* who are holding you back from living the life you deserve.

Yes, I'm totally serious. *Anyone. Maybe all of them.*

If you love yourself, toxic people have got to go.

Don't get me wrong: I'm not talking about ditching friends and family members because you get into a typical disagreement, the kind we all have with others from time to time. You know, like, *"Hey, I don't want to go to Applebee's, let's go to Fridays."* That isn't holding you back from living a happy, healthy life (unless you insist on having the brisket, which too much of can indeed kill you). It's the normal negotiations we all have with one another.

No one gives a fuck about that shit.

And, to be clear: I'm not talking about getting rid of people because they doubt you or are skeptical of an idea you have—not everyone will support your dreams, any more than you support every idea someone throws at you.

But the people who attack you physically or emotionally, damage your self-esteem and/or refuse to support *any* of your dreams? There's only one word that fits, and that word is:

Gone.

The people who tell you you're not worthy of great things, tell you that you're undeserving of having more, and go out of their way to *sabotage your dreams* in devious ways? *They have to fucking go.*

The soul-crushing, bring-nothing-good-into-your-life leeches who suck your time and energy...

Gone.

The narcissistic, self-serving and psychologically destructive assholes who love themselves so much they don't have the ability to love anyone else...

Gone. Gone.

The people who hate themselves so much they find it impossible to love you...

Gone. Gone. Gone.

Or the ex-husband who hates you more than he loves his children (yes, I had one of those, too)...

Pack-the-fucking-truck gone.

And if someone decides to cut me from their life, I don't get all bent about it. If I have the right to cut people from my life that don't serve my goals and dreams, then others have the same right.

Everything Toxic Is Out

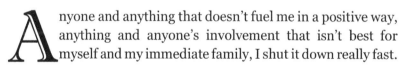

Anyone and anything that doesn't fuel me in a positive way, anything and anyone's involvement that isn't best for myself and my immediate family, I shut it down really fast.

Sometimes, when I'm coaching someone, they'll say something that comes across defensive and quickly apologize. That's okay, no harm, no foul. But if someone says something evil or deeply offensive, I cut them loose faster than you can say Bibbidi-Bobbidi-Fuck-You.

The same goes for the wrong kind of news and entertainment. Anyone who is mean, superficial or gossipy, I shut it down right away. And if I can't shut it down, they're out. Or I am.

Your heart knows when something or someone isn't good for you. So fucking listen to it!

Other Things to Avoid

Here's a short list of other things to avoid—things that are clearly toxic for bitches who want to create a fairytale kingdom:

- Politics (especially if paying attention to it puts you in a state of constant rage)
- Celebrity breakups and/or celebrity deaths
- Death in general, celebrity or otherwise
- Hurricane coverage, earthquake footage, villages engulfed in mud, etc.
- Terrorism, foreign or domestic
- (Speaking of terrorism) Most social media, especially Instagram and Twitter (unless you need it for business, and then the less the better)
- Stories about freak accidents, no matter how interesting they are
- Just about everything that happens in Florida, tune it out
- Bad friends, bad job, bad hair
- Complaining, jealousy, stress, sulfates, parabens (and if you happen to have a 55-gallon drums of *RoundUp*® laying around)...

...it's all got to go.

Sever Toxic Relationships

Loving yourself means digging deep to find the inner-bitch courage you need to sever toxic relationships that aren't serving you. No hate, no anger, but from a place of love for yourself, but also with love for them.

You can still love them, even if you need to let them go.

I have a sister I haven't talked to in years because of the negative effect she has on my life and my goals. And there are others I have been forced to shut out, as well.

My mother and I went a long time without talking. During our first phone call in years, she ended up proving her toxic self to me once again.

The minute I said hello, she proceeded to cuss me out. I'm all about the f-bomb, bitches. I sprinkle that shit around like confetti—but this was over the top.

But she said the things she did for no other purpose than to hurt, belittle, control. *To damage.*

During that call, my mother made it explicitly clear that her life was none of my fucking business. She gave me no choice but to agree.

A few blocked phone numbers and social media profiles later, my life wasn't her business anymore, either.

I booted her.

My life, my choice.

Your choice, your life, too. Family doesn't get to *make the cut* simply because they share your share DNA.

Not if you love yourself enough.

What About Prince Charming?

But what if the toxic family member in question is your Prince Charming? Am I advocating divorce? Not necessarily. But in certain cases?

Fuck yeah.

If your Prince Charming is toxic, he's no prince—and he certainly isn't *charming*. And if your prince stops being your prince and becomes a douche bag, the same rule applies. He's got to go—or you've got to go, depending on the situation.

If you love yourself, just walk away.

With nothing, if necessary.

As long as you leave with your soul and self-respect, you've got everything you need to start over. Everything else can be replaced.

I know this all too well.

I divorced the same guy twice, remember?

Don't misread what I'm saying. I'm NOT saying you should leave (or threaten to leave) every time your guy leaves the toilet seat up. But there are extreme cases where marriages *should* end.

Must end.

Have to end.

If this is you, you already know it.

You *do* know it, right?

Branden's Magical Maxim #7
for Manifesting a Fairytale Life:

Love yourself so hard you have an abundance to share with others.

#OUATB

I have personal goals and individual plans, but I also have a husband to please, kids to raise, and a household to balance. I have a business to run and books to write. I'm constantly battling the bulge hanging over my mom jeans and often feel like I need Spanx for my Spanx.

Let it suffice to say, I'm busy.

Some days I am *so* busy I have to choose between *me* eating or my four-year-old getting her lunch. I've got a lot of balls in the air and am in a constant state of trying to keep my shit together. Actually, I don't think anyone truly has their shit together—not entirely—and if you think they do, it's only because they've become great at fooling others.

So how do I cope, survive and (sometimes) thrive? I start with the most important, non-negotiable parts of my day. As much as I wish I could skip sitting in the pickup line at school and let my kids find their own way home, this is non-negotiable. I've done this task twice a day, five times a week, for years. Sometimes I actually try to convince myself they can manage and figure out how to get home on their own, then I quickly come to my senses and grab the car keys.

Living in this hectic, modern world—one that expects so much of us and from us—who we are and what we are can easily disappear.

That's why we must learn to love ourselves first.

Do you know who I love more than anyone else in the world? The answer is me.

I love myself.

I'll go so far as to say that the relationship I have with myself trumps everything else in my life. *Everything*. It comes before the relationship I have with my husband.

And with my children.

And even my relationship with God.

I know what you're probably thinking: *Branden, you couldn't possibly mean that!* Yes, I do. I believe God loves me more when I love myself. He certainly didn't create us with the intent of having us hate ourselves, right? Of course not.

I also work on loving myself first because the relationship I have with myself is the one I have taken for granted the most. And if the relationship I have with myself isn't one of *self-love*, the chances of having full and loving relationships with my husband, kids and/or God is near zero.

At some point in your day, your number-one priority is to spend some time loving yourself. Looking in the mirror and loving the powerful bitch that stares back at you. Yes, that's the priority over your children, your husband, your Bible study class—any and all of it. It all starts with loving yourself. *You* loving *you* is everything. That should be the top on your list of priorities. Put *your* mask on first (if you don't know what that means, Google it).

Loving Yourself Is Loving Others

You might *say* you love the people in your life, but if you don't truly love yourself—who you *really* are—your ability to love others fully and completely is total bullshit. Yes, this includes your husband and your children. If you don't love who *you* are, you are no good to anyone.

You can argue with me here if you want, but I'm telling you: Until you figure out who you are and start putting yourself first, you will never understand the power I am talking about.

If you find it hard to love yourself because you think it's selfish, then don't do it for yourself—do it for the people around you, for your husband/partner, your family, your children. Do it for your friends and co-workers. Because if you don't take care of yourself by loving yourself first, they'll be forced into the position of having to take care of you.

Do it for the sake of your goals, your hopes, your dreams. They need you to love yourself, too. Satisfaction, fulfillment and self-respect are all related to self-love.

Forgive Yourself for Everything

I'm not perfect. I've got my own bag of shit, and sometimes my shit is a lot for others to take. But you still have to love yourself. It all starts there. Which means that, in addition to finding the strength to forgive others for the things they've done to you, you must also find the strength to forgive yourself for your own shit.

One of the side benefits I discovered when I set out on my self-love journey was how I automatically began to forgive myself for things I'd previously had so much guilt over. I found myself accepting of my flaws and shortcomings, not hating myself for them.

Forgiveness isn't only something you do for others, it's also a gift you give yourself. I've not only forgiven my mother and my sister and my ex-husband for the crap they dished on me, but I've also forgiven myself for my part in it and everything else I've fucked up. It took a long time to realize I could use the power of forgiveness to forgive myself.

- *For hurting others along the way...*
- *For my dumb decisions...*
- *And for being human.*

I destroyed an entire kingdom once, and my family is still paying that price. Divorce is ugly when kids are involved, a process filled with shame, devastation, disappointment, humiliation, heartbreak and more. There simply are not enough adjectives in the world to describe the pain and emotions involved. I know that leaving was the right thing to do, yet I beat myself up over it every day for years. I still cringe just talking about it.

Forgive yourself for all of it. *All of it.* Every last fucking bit of it, no matter how horrible. Yes, some of the fucked-up shit you've done is by definition "unforgivable"...

Forgive yourself anyway.

Controlling "Self-Talk"

A big part of loving yourself is controlling what you say to yourself. I'm talking about your inner critic—that fucking voice in your head that constantly judges you. Belittles and doubts you. The voice that's intent on telling you that you're not good enough, tall enough, thin enough, pretty enough, smart enough, loveable enough.

The voice tells you that you're stupid and unworthy. It tells you you'll never succeed. That your goals are unattainable—not for everyone, others can reach them, just not you. Worse, it says things specifically designed to hurt—things that are so nasty and vile you would never think of saying them to another human being—but you'll say them to yourself.

That shit has got to stop.

I've come to the conclusion that it's not what other people say about you that matters, *it's what you say to yourself that counts.* I can't tell you how many years I looked in the mirror and criticized myself about every part of me I hated.

I still catch myself every now and then staring at C-section number six, the folds of my stomach hanging over my stretch marks—telling myself I look like someone who gave birth to and nursed six babies, while suffering from an Oreo addiction—instead of seeing the beauty in what my body was capable of doing, birthing and nurturing six fabulous kids.

The mirror wasn't my friend.

Even deeper than that (outside appearance, extra weight and saggy breasts aside), I hated who I was as a person. My habit of yo-yo dieting combined with my ridiculous eating habits was bad enough, but the way I fed my mind and soul a never-ending diet of criticism and negativity was even worse.

I not only thought that I was ugly, but my thoughts were ugly. I felt I had nothing to be proud of, so my mind filled me with feelings of hatred and self-loathing. I didn't even know who I was anymore. Or how I'd gotten there.

When I used to look in the mirror, the only thing I saw looking back at me was a lost little girl—lost, lost, lost—like a slipper that got dropped while racing for the carriage at midnight.

Illogical Logic

The more I hated myself, the worse the decisions I made. I got comfortable punishing myself day in and day out. Eventually I simply avoided the mirror altogether. I ate my feelings and hoped that by putting on my make-up or fixing my hair, I could hide my self-loathing.

I was not a wife to be proud of, and even crankier as a mom. I was just miserable. Life was fucking hard, and I wasn't making it any easier punishing myself for ridiculous reasons. I was building a wall of weight to push people away. In my fucked-up mind I felt that if I was fat enough, I could give everyone a reason to be disgusted with me. Then, when I was rejected, it wouldn't hurt so bad. I was pushing everyone away with circular, fucked-up logic.

Logic that wasn't logical at all.

Even when I was working out with a personal trainer, eating healthier, I still hated myself. Still found all of the flaws and continued on the cycle of self-loathing. Every excuse I had to stay depressed and miserable, I took it.

I was trapped in a prison of my own making.

Locking Yourself in the Tower

If you look for excuses to stay where you are, the excuses always appear. They're not real, of course, they're simply things *you* manufacture to stay stuck.

Because there's a part of us that likes staying stuck. We hate being stuck, but it's comfortable at the same time. Feeling stuck means not having to change.

It's comfortable to doubt yourself, your abilities, your self-worth—especially when all you've done for years is send yourself those messages.

If this describes you, don't feel defective. It describes everyone to some degree. For some people it's their weight, for others it's their nose. For others still it's their intelligence or lack thereof. Everybody's got something they beat themselves up over.

Everybody.

The problem is there's a part of us that likes it.

This is very normal, and yes it fucking sucks. And as much as I wish I could help you get the time back that you wasted beating yourself up, I can't. That's water under the bridge. That ship has sailed. (Insert the water analogy of your choice here.) But I sure as fuck can tell you that it's time to embrace a new mindset, new perception, and new reality going forward.

Stop making excuses as to why you shouldn't come first. Love yourself the way you imagine a princess would.

Whose Voice Is It?

It's tempting to think the voice you're hearing is yours, which, of course, it is. *Then again, maybe it isn't.* At least it's not your deepest, most authentic voice. Not the voice you used to hear when you were young, before you started buying into the world's bullshit.

Do you even remember that voice—the one that thought anything was possible? Do you remember that voice? The one you used to hear when you were young? The voice that thought that if you flapped your arms hard enough you could fly to the moon?

That's you. *That's fucking you.*

The voice you hear in your head today is a collection of expectations, doubts and limitations gathered and curated by your inner critic. The problem is that you've been listening to that voice for so long now, you *think* the voice is yours.

It's not.

The voice you've been listening to hasn't been yours for a very long time. You only think it's yours.

And make no mistake: the voice in your head is probably not your friend. *The majority of the time, it's your enemy.* The voice is a schoolyard bully, demanding your lunch money and stealing your pride and self-esteem with it. And, like with any bully, I thought I'd try and ignore it.

I quickly learned it wasn't enough to simply ignore the voice. It couldn't be ignored.

So I tried reasoning with it: *"Leave me alone,"* I said. The voice laughed and said, *"No." "Please, just leave me alone!"* I said with tears rolling down my cheeks. The bully-voice smiled and said, *"Make me."*

That's when I realized there are only three ways to deal with a bully:

1. *Ignore the bully and hope they go away.*

2. *Beg, plead and try to reason with them.*

3. *Punch the fucker in the nose.*

I've tried option #1 and option #2 without success.

So I decided to fight back.

The Loudest Voice Wins

Fighting back against the voice became my mission. The question was, how? How do you fight an enemy that has had an outpost in your head for years? An enemy that knows everything about you—your every fear and weakness—with a lifetime of experience and practice dominating your every thought? It felt hopeless, like David fighting Goliath.

The first thing I did was decide that if the voice in my head was going to bully me by calling me names, I could do the same thing to it. So I gave the bully-voice a name. I decided to call it *The Evil Witch*. Giving the voice a name:

- *Made it easier to see the voice was not my friend, and...*

- *Let me make fun of it rather than allowing it to make fun of me.*

From that moment on, I simply started telling the voice to go fuck itself.

- The voice would say, *"You're so stupid, Branden,"* to which I would respond, *"No, you're stupid you Evil Witch, go fuck yourself."*

- The voice would say, *"Look at yourself, Branden, see those stretch marks? You're hideous, unlovable,"* to which I would respond, *"No, you're the Evil Hag, not me. Go shove your broomstick where the sun doesn't shine."*

- The voice would say, *"Give it up, Branden, you're never going to be a published author,"* to which I would respond, *"Oh, yeah, just watch me toothless motherfucker."*

At first, I had to scream at the voice when it started in with its bullshit criticisms and belittlement, using volume to overcome it. Later, I could counteract it with a normal voice volume. Eventually, I could whisper it away.

The voice wasn't gone, not entirely. It never fully went away, but it was quieter. Less frequent. It had become a salesperson who'd finally learned to pass by my door because I wasn't buying any more of her bullshit.

Then I had my final breakthrough. I thought: *What if rather than just trying to shut the voice up, maybe I could actually change what it was saying?*

Wouldn't *that* be cool?

Positive Affirmations

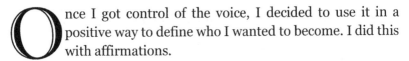Once I got control of the voice, I decided to use it in a positive way to define who I wanted to become. I did this with affirmations.

Did I mention I have taken over our house? All of it. I have an office in every room and I have rearranged my husband and the kids to fit my needs. And there are construction paper notes plastered all over the walls, telling my prince and my kids that I love them and reminding them to pick up their shit.

I also write love notes to myself. Yes, I write love notes to myself, reminding me how much I love myself—lest I forget.

- *I am strong...*
- *I am brave...*
- *I am fearless...*
- *I am independent...*
- *I am love...*
- *I am positive energy...*
- *I am deserving of more...*
- *I am a magnet for abundance...*
- *The universe has my back...*

And on and on and on.

Using affirmations feels silly at first, which is why so few people will use them. But they work.

Trust me, they work.

Affirmations are your way of defining who you are for yourself, as well as who you will become.

Note: I'm not going to use space here listing all the affirmations I use, but if you want you can download my list of *"77 Bitchingly Positive Affirmations for Achieving a Fairytale Life"* at:
www.BrandenLaNette.com/Affirmations

Loving Your Body

I'd be guilty of motivational malpractice if I didn't highlight the negative self-image most of us have about our bodies. And the thought is this:

The self-image we have of our bodies should be just that—a *self*-image, one *we* decide on for our*selves*—*ours and ours alone*. What anyone else (aka, "society") thinks about us is nothing more than an opinion and totally irrelevant. So, if someone says something negative about your looks, your weight or whatever—whether it's to your face, behind your back, or on social media—you have my permission to tell them to suck a dick.

It's your body, not theirs—you're the one who has to live with it, so why do they even care? The answer is simple: It's because they don't like their own body. They don't love themselves and probably never will. Someone's got to break the cycle, so you do it—you break the cycle. You fall in love with you. You don't have to be a cover girl model to be beautiful.

I am so damn happy with that beautiful creature staring back at me today, I really am. I'm not trying to sell you on this, and I certainly am not trying to sell myself. The love I have for myself is deep, it's real, but it didn't happen overnight. It required years of small self-love-habits, done consistently—finding power and celebration in small wins every day—until the change stuck.

Find your fucking power.

You are beautiful, you are worthy, you are enough.

Just the way you are.

But...

You can always be better.

Yes, I know—it's a total mind-fuck.

You are perfect, just the way you are...
but you can always be better?

On the surface it sounds like a contradiction, but it's not. As one of my teachers , Wayne Dyer, said (again, I'm paraphrasing):

> *Go outside and look at the sky and see how perfect it is. Then, go outside a few hours from now and see how different the sky is—it's totally different, yet it's still perfect.*

Even at your worst, you are perfect. And later, at your best, you will be perfect, too.

- *It's all in how you see things...*
- *In how you talk to yourself...*
- *In what you choose to focus on...*
- *In the story you choose to tell yourself.*

Stories are like tools in a toolbox. The only question is, which stories do you want to use? And what meaning do you want to give them?

In the same amount of time it takes to use your stories to destroy your life and your future, you could use the *exact same stories* to get everything you *do* want.

Every story you need to get what you want is available in your mind, there for the thinking. And every story you need to use as an excuse for *not* getting what you want is available, too. Sometimes it's the same fucking story, it only depends on *how* you want to use it.

You've got to choose which side you want to be on—the side that looks for reasons to get the life you want, or the side that looks for reasons you can't.

There is no *"in between."* One side or the other.

Pick.

You can choose to use the events in your past stories as reasons you can do something (as motivation) or reasons you can't (as excuses.) Same story. Different use. You choose.

It's up to you.

Want to Change Your Future?

The question now is—what's your life going to look like five years from now? Ten years from now? Twenty? Where will you be? What will you have? Who will you be? It will all come down to the choices you make.

Want to change your future?

Change the stories you tell yourself.

Want to change your past?

Change the way you think about the things that happened to you and find the power in those events.

Yes, your past is your past, and it can't be changed.

But how you think about it *can* be.

Congratufuckinglations, bitches!

You're just a few pages from finishing a book written specifically to help you spark the courage you need to create your fairytale life. And let me state categorically:

I am under no illusion that I have all the answers—hell, I'm not even sure I have all the questions.

I'm simply thrilled as fuck to have played a small part in your journey toward a better life, filled with the joy and happiness you deserve.

So let's wrap this puppy up with a few final thoughts...

My biggest struggle in life right now (besides changing diapers while simultaneously microwaving frozen burritos and typing these final words to this book) is knowing so many people are:

- *Waking up to lives they hate...*

- *Looking in the mirror at themselves with disgust...*

- *Allowing their past to dictate their futures...*

- *Struggling to make ends meet...*

- *Going to bed at night with a sense of emptiness and hopelessness...*

And, maybe worst of all, going through their days believing the world is *"out to get them."*

Recently my prince went to the basement in search of hinges for a cupboard door that should have fallen off years ago. When he turned on the light, he looked around the corner and saw water suddenly spraying all over the basement from our water heater. The old thing (the water heater, not my husband) was probably overdue to spring a leak, and he freaked out. He was exhausted, having just come off a week of mandatory overtime.

My husband's reaction was not a good one.

To make matters worse, fixing the cupboard door was a task within my husband's skill set—fixing the hot water heater was not. A repair man was required, which meant an unexpected expense for our budget.

After throwing an ugly tantrum, the repair man came and quickly fixed the problem. Total repair bill: *$125.*

Here's the thing:

Had the leak started at any other time, our basement would have totally flooded, and the result would have been far worse. Perhaps financially catastrophic. Instead of $125, we could have been on the hook for $4,000 or more for a water heater *and* flood repair.

The search for a hinge to repair a broken cupboard door led to the discovery of a potentially bigger problem at precisely the right time. My husband's overtime paid for the water heater repair, the repairman got some overtime for himself in the process, and our house was safe.

My husband's initial reaction was, *"Fuck, why is this happening to us?"*

I knew differently.

Slaying Dragons

Creating a fairytale life requires that we become dragon slayers, and to be clear: The dragon in this story is *not* the hot water heater. The dragon in this story is our minds.

Our *thinking.*

My husband was stressed and unhappy when he saw the water leak. *I was fascinated to watch the situation unfolding before us.*

He was angry because of what was happening *to* us. I was grateful because I knew better. I knew it was happening *for* us. Because the universe never does anything *to* us, it only does things *for* us.

Do you believe that? Do you believe that when even the worst comes your way that the universe has a plan? That it's acting in your best interest, even if the reason the thing is happening isn't immediately obvious?

No?

Maybe you should start.

Happiness and joy are not about what happens to you, but rather how you think, react and respond to what happens.

Develop an Abundance Mentality

Many people believe happiness and abundance are in short supply. They feel that to get more from life, they have to take something away from other people. This is just another mindfuck, another reason why you need to develop an abundance mentality.

You need to know right now that there is enough of everything in the world to make everyone's chalice runneth over—money, love, happiness, all of it—*without having to compete with anyone.* There is no competition, outside of yourself. The only person you need to worry about competing with is the person you were yesterday.

When you have a mindset full of lack, everyone is a threat. When you have a mindset of abundance, you're not only able to help yourself, you can also help other people shine. For example, If you've read this book and feel you can write a better one, fucking go do it. Seriously. Do it. I'll sharpen your pencil. For real. But understand this: *You won't be competing with me—you'll be competing with yourself.*

The same thing goes for blogging, starting a home-based business, being a singer, starting a restaurant, and on and on. It's a big world. There's room for everyone. Jump in and make a splash! Or don't. Which is fine, too. It's your life. Live it any way you fucking want to.

Having an abundance mindset means you never have to be a victim, that you believe in all possibilities. Say that out loud for fucks sake:

"I believe in all possibilities."

Wait, in fairytales you never say incantations and spells just once, you have to repeat them three times:

"I believe in all possibilities."

"I believe in all possibilities."

"I believe in all possibilities."

Feels good, doesn't it?

Your Fairytale Ending Awaits

We all have different dreams, hopes and aspirations. That's why I can promise you there is room for everyone at the top. What happens is not everyone feels like they deserve to be there. They use every stumbling block, every failed attempt, and lack of discipline as a reason to give up.

You're not going to do that, not anymore.

You are perfectly imperfect in all your own ways, and you are ready to take on your power and all the disciplines necessary to bring your life into an action of abundance.

Learn to give affection. And to receive affection, too. And, please, for the love of God, learn how to take a compliment. When someone says, *"I love your dress,"* don't respond with, *"Oh, it was on sale,"* or some other such deflective bullshit. Just smile and say thank you.

Having an abundance mindset leaves you feeling full, creative, inspired and free. It brings new opportunities and creates the possibility for meaningful experiences.

Life has the fairytale-ending option.

All you have to do is write it.

AFTERWORD BY
BENJAMIN

(a.k.a. "Prince Charming")

The foreword for this book was obviously meant to be written by a big-name, recognizable person. So let me start by thanking Ellen DeGeneres, Oprah Winfrey, Gary V, Molly Bloom, Tony Robbins, Jenna Kutcher, Rachel Hollis, and Mel Robbins for NOT writing the foreword Branden requested. It freed up a few pages for me to say a few things.

First, it's funny (and somewhat fitting) that, instead of this being in the front of the book, Branden has so graciously put me in the back. I wonder if that is something I need to get used to? Or maybe I haven't realized that this is the truth of my life, that I am destined to follow the leader.

My name is Benjamin, Branden LaNette's husband. I have been a part of the Branden show since a year to the day before we got married in Las Vegas. Yes, our wedding day, was all about Branden, in a wedding dress, running the streets and stages of Vegas. It was all we could do to keep up with her from one venue to the next. Fun times. It hasn't stopped since.

I'm so thankful for it.

Branden has many superpowers, chief among them being love and compassion. Both unconditional. This makes her an amazing mom. She is as beautiful on the inside as she is on the outside. She gives 100% to these kids and I've always admired her parenting— even found myself jealous at times. Anyone would want a mom like her. That's why she has been blessed with six. I knew there was no better way to tell you who she is than asking all six of our babies about their mom:

- Our 17-year-old, Shay, says: "Mom is irrational, stubborn, and defensive. She has flaws but she is inspiring, and loving, and caring. I wouldn't want anyone else for a mom. I am very thankful.

- Our 15-year-old, Jezra says: "Mom is crazy, loud, and proud. She's not afraid to say what she thinks and feels. It's a great life lesson, but at my age it's embarrassing—but she is always there to build us up, to push us to be our best, and to know we can do anything we want. There's no one in the world like her and she instills in us that things happen for us, not to us."

- Our 11-year-old, Malachi, says: "Blueberry muffins." If you follow Branden it would make sense. He also says if she was ever up for sale, he would buy all of her. I know he adores his mom. This kid is magic when it comes to being loving, just like her.

- Our 9-year-old Isaiah said, "Mom is really doing good, she's running a business, she has a book coming out, she's just doing really great things. She wants us to love our dreams. She says never give up." Another reflection of his mom. The one that looks most like her too.

- Our 4-year-old Zaden said she loves mommy for taking her to the Y and dance class at PIM, taking her on bike rides and to the park. I can say she loves sleeping next to her mama every night more than anything.

- Finally, there's Alexandria, our youngest. Branden literally won't put her down for several more months. That's how it goes with all of her children. They are stuck to her for the first one and a half to two years. The woman doesn't pee without Alexandria, and I'm not exaggerating. That Alexandria would choose her mom over anyone else in the world is the biggest compliment that can be given. No *quote* beyond that is necessary.

When Branden told me she wanted to write this book on top of parenting our children, running a business and running the household, my first thought was that the laundry pile was not going away anytime soon. And it didn't. None of us are the worse for it.

I sometimes feel like that kid being dragged through the store because I don't walk fast enough, because she is always very forward thinking and motivated on what's next. I've always believed in her magic so I support her.

And it can be a little stressful because I've always been a *"live to be comfortable"* guy, that's not her jam, and even in her bad days, when she is crying and wanting to throw in the towel, I find strength in the things I've learned from her. I tell her what she always tells me, that we'll stick it out—that everything will work out for us—and it always does.

There is little I would change about Branden, other than having to force date night on her to keep the foundation between the two of us strong. And if there was such a thing as a fairy godmother who could grant me a wish, it would be to change her taste in music. She likes everything, which unfortunately includes rap.

One key thing I've learned about Branden is that she needs to hear words of affirmation from me more often (don't we all?) which happens to be one of my biggest weaknesses. Her only weakness is that she's terrified of frogs. Good thing I was her prince, cause she sure as hell wasn't going to kiss anything else.

To wrap up here, let me say that The Branden Show *is* magic, and I'm forever grateful for tuning in. And I'm proud of her for sharing her true heart in this book. We will *all* be better for it. From your biggest fan, great job babe. You are the only person who could find a prince inside my soul.

Love, Benjamin

About the Author...

BRANDEN LaNETTE doesn't look like a typical author, but she has long ignored what she "should" do, say and look like. On her own at a very young age, Branden eventually found herself with the wrong guy, the wrong job, and a bleak future. The fairytale she was promised as a child never materialized.

Finally, Branden decided that she wanted something different for her life and realized no one was going to do it for her. Prince charming wasn't coming to save her—she'd have to save herself.

Step by step, decision by decision, through major trials and tribulations that would stop most people in their tracks, Branden learned how to turn heartbreak into happiness <u>and</u> self-judgement into inner joy.

Today, Branden LaNette is an entrepreneur, coach, speaker, wife, and stay-at-home Mom to six C-section babies (ages 1-16) and way too many f-ing pets. Somehow, however, she manages to juggle all of this effortlessly (a blatant lie) while pushing her way through the kinds of fear and self-doubts that whisper within all of us (totally true) to achieve her goals. Her most recent dream come true is this book, one that is destined to have a major impact on millions of women across the globe (or at least nine people in Michigan.)

Through it all, she has found her happiness, her joy—*and her unique voice.*

Let's Connect, Bitches!

Facebook: Branden.Lanette

Instagram: @Brandenlanettel

Twitter: @Branden_LaNette

Oh, don't forget, visit me at:
OnceUponATimeBitches.com

Finally... Thank you so much for reading.
You are part of my dream come true.

Is now an okay time to ask for a favor?

I would LOVE and greatly appreciate if you would consider leaving an honest review of my book on your favorite book buying platform.